THE AUSTRALIAN
Women's Weekly

I'm a firm believer in what goes around, comes around, and French food, one of my all-time favourite cuisines, has done exactly that. The swing of the culinary pendulum has seen French food arc back from the 1970s and sweep onto today's restaurant and kitchen tables. Gathering the ideas for *New French Food* was not just a mouth-watering experience, but also a lot of fun as we came up with modern twists on classic recipes and checked out the latest influences on bistro dining. Bon appétit!

Pamela Clark

Food Director

contents

soups and starters

onion soup with gruyère croûtons

PREPARATION TIME 30 MINUTES **COOKING TIME** 50 MINUTES

50g butter
4 large brown onions (800g), halved, sliced thinly
¾ cup (180ml) dry white wine
3 cups (750ml) water
1 litre (4 cups) beef stock
1 bay leaf
1 tablespoon plain flour
1 teaspoon fresh thyme leaves
1 small french bread stick
1 cup (125g) finely grated gruyère cheese

1 Melt butter in large saucepan; cook onion, stirring occasionally, over medium heat, about 30 minutes or until caramelised.
2 Meanwhile, bring wine to a boil in medium saucepan; boil 1 minute. Stir in the water, stock and bay leaf; return to a boil. Remove from heat.
3 Stir flour into onion mixture; cook, stirring, until mixture bubbles and thickens. Gradually add hot stock mixture, stirring until mixture boils and thickens slightly. Reduce heat; simmer soup, uncovered, stirring occasionally, 20 minutes. Discard bay leaf; stir in thyme.
4 Meanwhile, cut bread into 1.5cm slices; discard end pieces. Toast slices on one side under preheated grill. Turn slices; top each with about 1 tablespoon of the cheese; grill croûtons until cheese melts.
5 Divide soup among serving bowls; top with croûtons, sprinkle with remaining cheese.

serves 4
per serving 22.3g fat; 1761kJ (421 cal)

creamy watercress soup

PREPARATION TIME 30 MINUTES **COOKING TIME** 30 MINUTES

1 tablespoon olive oil
1 small brown onion (80g), chopped finely
1 small leek (200g), sliced thinly
3 medium potatoes (600g), chopped coarsely
1 litre (4 cups) chicken stock
350g watercress, trimmed
⅓ cup (80g) sour cream

1 Heat oil in large saucepan; cook onion and leek, stirring over low heat, until vegetables soften. Add potato and stock; bring to a boil. Reduce heat; simmer, covered, about 20 minutes or until potato is almost tender.
2 Reserve four watercress sprigs; stir remaining watercress into pan. Simmer soup, uncovered, about 5 minutes or until potato is tender.
3 Blend or process soup, in batches, until smooth. Reheat soup in same pan then divide among serving bowls; top each with 1 tablespoon of the sour cream then a reserved watercress sprig.

serves 4
per serving 14.1g fat; 1075kJ (257 cal)

white bean, leek and garlic sausage soup

PREPARATION TIME 30 MINUTES (PLUS STANDING TIME)   **COOKING TIME** I HOUR I5 MINUTES

Haricot, great northern, cannellini or navy beans can be used in this
recipe. Merguez sausages, from North Africa, are traditionally made with
lamb and seasoned with garlic and hot spices. They can be found at
most delicatessens and butchers. Pistou, from the south of France, is
very similar to Italian pesto, and is usually stirred into hot soup at the table
so that the aroma enlivens the diner's palate.

1 cup (200g) dried small
    white beans
40g butter
2 bacon rashers (140g), rind
    removed, chopped finely
2 cloves garlic, crushed
1 medium leek (350g),
    sliced thinly
2 trimmed celery stalks (200g),
    chopped finely
2 medium carrots (240g),
    chopped finely
1.5 litres (6 cups) chicken stock
1 bay leaf
4 merguez sausages (320g)

PISTOU
2 cups loosely packed fresh
    basil leaves
1 clove garlic, quartered
¼ cup (20g) coarsely grated
    parmesan cheese
¼ cup (60ml) extra virgin
    olive oil

1 Place beans in medium bowl, cover with water; soak overnight, drain.
   Rinse under cold water; drain.
2 Melt butter in large saucepan; cook bacon, garlic, leek, celery and
   carrot, stirring, until vegetables soften. Stir in stock, bay leaf and
   beans; bring to a boil. Reduce heat; simmer soup, covered, about
   1 hour or until beans are tender.
3 Meanwhile, make pistou.
4 Heat medium non-stick frying pan; cook sausages until browned.
   Drain on absorbent paper; chop coarsely.
5 Just before serving, ladle soup into serving bowls; top with sausage
   and a spoonful of pistou.

PISTOU   Blend or process ingredients until smooth.

serves 6
per serving 28.3g fat; 1577kJ (377 cal)

roasted parsnip and garlic soup

PREPARATION TIME 25 MINUTES **COOKING TIME** 1 HOUR 20 MINUTES

1 garlic bulb
2 tablespoons olive oil
1kg parsnips, chopped coarsely
1 tablespoon olive oil, extra
1 small brown onion (80g),
    chopped finely
1 medium potato (200g),
    chopped coarsely
1 litre (4 cups) chicken stock
300ml cream
¾ cup (180ml) milk
2 tablespoons finely chopped
    fresh garlic chives

ANCHOVY TOASTS

6 anchovy fillets, drained,
    chopped finely
2 tablespoons finely chopped
    fresh garlic chives
50g butter, softened
1 small french bread stick

1 Preheat oven to moderately hot.
2 Place whole unpeeled garlic bulb in large shallow baking dish; roast, uncovered, in moderately hot oven 10 minutes. Add combined oil and parsnip; roast, uncovered, in moderately hot oven about 30 minutes or until garlic and parsnip are tender. When garlic is cool enough to handle, halve garlic bulb crossways; use fingers to squeeze garlic puree into small bowl. Reserve.
3 Heat extra oil in large saucepan; cook onion, stirring, until softened. Add parsnip with potato and stock; bring to a boil. Reduce heat; simmer soup, uncovered, stirring occasionally, about 20 minutes or until potato is softened.
4 Meanwhile, make anchovy toasts.
5 Blend or process soup with reserved garlic puree, in batches, until smooth. Reheat soup in same pan, stir in cream and milk; bring to a boil. Ladle soup into serving bowls; sprinkle with chives. Serve soup with anchovy toasts.

ANCHOVY TOASTS Combine anchovy, chives and butter in small bowl. Cut bread into 1.5cm slices; discard end pieces. Toast slices on one side under preheated grill. Turn slices; spread each with anchovy mixture; grill until anchovy mixture bubbles.

serves 4
per serving 56.8g fat; 3261kJ (779 cal)

TIP When peeling the parsnips, make sure you remove all of the bitter outer layer.

fish and fennel soup

PREPARATION TIME 30 MINUTES **COOKING TIME** 35 MINUTES

We used ling here, but you can use any fish you like as long as it's firm enough not to break up during cooking.

1 tablespoon olive oil
1 large brown onion (200g), chopped coarsely
1 medium fennel bulb (300g), trimmed, chopped coarsely
2 cloves garlic, crushed
3 cups (750ml) fish stock
1 cup (250ml) dry white wine
6 medium tomatoes (900g), peeled, chopped finely
500g firm white fish fillets
¼ cup coarsely chopped fresh flat-leaf parsley

1 Heat oil in medium saucepan; cook onion, fennel and garlic, stirring occasionally, until vegetables soften. Add stock, wine and about two-thirds of the tomato; bring to a boil. Reduce heat; simmer soup, uncovered, stirring occasionally, 10 minutes.
2 Add fish to soup; simmer, covered, about 15 minutes or until cooked through. Remove fish from soup; flake fish with fork, divide among serving bowls.
3 Blend or process soup, in batches, until smooth. Reheat soup in same pan; stir in parsley. Ladle soup into serving bowls; top with fish and remaining tomato.

serves 4
per serving 8g fat; 1152kJ (275 cal)

salmon and green peppercorn rillettes

PREPARATION TIME 20 MINUTES **COOKING TIME** 20 MINUTES (PLUS COOLING TIME)

Traditionally, rillettes are similar to confit in that both are made of meat (usually pork) or poultry (usually duck) slowly cooked in seasoned fat; however, confit is generally preserved whole or in large pieces in its own fat while rillettes are pounded into a rough paste and potted before serving with toast or sliced bread. Here, we've used salmon fillets and added smoked salmon for a modern take on the traditional appetiser.

1 long french bread stick
3 cups (750ml) water
½ cup (125ml) dry white wine
1 small brown onion (80g), chopped coarsely
1 bay leaf
1 teaspoon black peppercorns
300g salmon fillets
100g smoked salmon, sliced thinly
60g butter, softened
2 teaspoons finely grated lemon rind
1 tablespoon green peppercorns in brine, rinsed,
    drained, chopped coarsely

1 Preheat oven to moderately slow.
2 Cut bread into 1cm slices; toast, uncovered, in single layer on oven tray in moderately slow oven about 15 minutes or until bread is dry.
3 Meanwhile, combine the water, wine, onion, bay leaf and black peppercorns in medium saucepan; bring to a boil. Add salmon fillets, reduce heat; simmer, uncovered, about 5 minutes or until almost cooked through. Remove from heat, cool salmon fillets in liquid 5 minutes then drain; discard cooking liquid.
4 Discard any skin and bones from salmon fillets; place in medium bowl, flake with fork. Add smoked salmon, butter, rind and green peppercorns; stir to combine rillettes. Divide rillettes among four ½-cup (125ml) dishes; cool to room temperature. Serve with bread slices.

serves 4
per serving 21.6g fat; 2025kJ (484 cal)

duck liver parfait with red onion jam

PREPARATION TIME 25 MINUTES **COOKING TIME** 40 MINUTES (PLUS REFRIGERATION TIME)

Shallots, also called french shallots, golden shallots or eschalots, are small, elongated members of the onion family that grow in tight clusters, similar to garlic.

30g butter
6 shallots (150g), chopped finely
2 cloves garlic, crushed
½ teaspoon ground allspice
1 tablespoon finely chopped
   fresh thyme
1 teaspoon cracked black pepper
⅔ cup (160ml) brandy
400g duck livers, trimmed
¾ cup (180ml) cream
4 eggs
150g butter, melted, cooled
2 bay leaves, halved
2 sprigs thyme, halved
100g butter, extra

RED ONION JAM

50g butter
4 medium red onions (680g),
   sliced thinly
¼ cup (55g) sugar
¾ cup (180ml) dry red wine
¼ cup (60ml) port
¼ cup (60ml) red wine vinegar

1 Preheat oven to slow.
2 Melt butter in small frying pan; cook shallot and garlic, stirring, until shallot softens. Add allspice, thyme, pepper and brandy; bring to a boil. Reduce heat; simmer, uncovered, about 2 minutes or until liquid is reduced to about 1 tablespoon.
3 Blend or process shallot mixture with livers, cream, eggs and melted butter until mixture is smooth. Push parfait mixture through fine sieve into medium bowl; repeat process through same cleaned sieve.
4 Pour parfait mixture into greased 1.5-litre (6-cup) ovenproof terrine dish; place terrine in baking dish. Pour enough boiling water into baking dish to come halfway up sides of terrine; cover terrine with foil. Cook, covered, in slow oven about 40 minutes or until liver parfait is just set. Remove terrine from baking dish; cool parfait 10 minutes.
5 Meanwhile, make red onion jam.
6 Decorate parfait with bay leaves and thyme. Melt extra butter in small pan; cool 2 minutes then carefully pour butter fat over parfait, leaving milk solids in pan. Cover parfait in terrine; refrigerate 3 hours or overnight.
7 Turn parfait onto board. Using hot, wet knife, cut parfait into eight slices; serve with red onion jam and, if desired, toasted brioche.

RED ONION JAM Melt butter in large frying pan; cook onion and sugar, stirring occasionally, over medium heat, about 20 minutes or until onion starts to caramelise. Add wine, port and vinegar; bring to a boil. Reduce heat; simmer, uncovered, about 30 minutes or until jam thickens.

serves 8
per serving 51.8g fat; 3535kJ (845 cal)

TIP Parfait and jam will keep up to four days, covered separately, in the refrigerator.

Push liver mixture through fine sieve into medium bowl.

Pour liver mixture into greased ovenproof terrine dish.

Pour water into baking dish to come halfway up sides of terrine.

caramelised onion and beetroot tart

PREPARATION TIME 20 MINUTES (PLUS FREEZING TIME) **COOKING TIME** 45 MINUTES

50g butter

4 medium red onions (680g), halved,
  sliced thinly

1 tablespoon red wine vinegar

1 teaspoon fresh thyme leaves

3 medium beetroot (500g), trimmed

1 sheet ready-rolled butter
  puff pastry

cooking-oil spray

120g baby rocket leaves

CHIVE OIL

½ cup coarsely chopped
  fresh chives

¾ cup (180ml) olive oil

1 ice cube

HORSERADISH CREAM

¾ cup (180ml) cream

1 tablespoon horseradish cream

1 Melt butter in medium frying pan; cook onion, stirring occasionally, over medium heat about 30 minutes or until caramelised. Stir in vinegar and thyme.

2 Meanwhile, boil, steam or microwave unpeeled beetroot until just tender; drain. When cool enough to handle, peel then slice beetroot thinly.

3 Preheat oven to hot.

4 Place pastry sheet on flat surface; cut a 24cm circle out of pastry. Place on oiled oven tray, prick all over with fork; freeze 10 minutes. Bake, uncovered, in hot oven about 5 minutes or until browned lightly.

5 Make chive oil. Make horseradish cream.

6 Spread onion mixture over pastry; top with slightly overlapping beetroot slices. Spray tart lightly with oil; bake, uncovered, in hot oven 10 minutes.

7 Meanwhile, combine rocket in medium bowl with half of the chive oil; divide among serving plates.

8 Cut tart into six wedges. Place each wedge on rocket, drizzle with remaining chive oil; serve with horseradish cream.

CHIVE OIL Blend or process ingredients until smooth.
HORSERADISH CREAM Beat cream in small bowl with electric mixer until soft peaks form; fold in horseradish cream.

serves 6
per serving 52.7g fat; 2436kJ (582 cal)

scallops with fennel and pernod sauce

PREPARATION TIME 20 MINUTES **COOKING TIME** 30 MINUTES

Pernod is an anise-flavoured liqueur drunk straight, or diluted with ice or water, as an aperitif. The French also call it pastis, and it is an extremely popular drink consumed in late afternoon as an appetite stimulant. When trimming the fennel bulbs reserve some of the frond tips to use to garnish the scallops.

24 scallops, on the half shell (600g)
60g butter
2 medium fennel bulbs (600g), trimmed, sliced thinly
4 green onions, sliced thinly
⅓ cup (80ml) pernod
300ml cream
1 tablespoon coarsely chopped fennel frond tips

1 Remove scallops from shells; wash shells, dry thoroughly, reserve.
2 Melt two-thirds of the butter in large frying pan; cook fennel, in batches, stirring occasionally, about 20 minutes or until softened.
3 Heat remaining butter in same pan; cook onion, stirring, until soft. Return fennel to pan with scallops, pernod and cream; cook about 2 minutes or until scallops are opaque.
4 Divide shells among serving plates. Using slotted spoon, transfer scallops to scallop shells. Reduce heat under sauce; simmer, stirring, until sauce thickens slightly. Spoon sauce over scallops; sprinkle with frond tips.

serves 6
per serving 27.4g fat; 1559kJ (372 cal)

oysters with leek confit and salmon roe

PREPARATION TIME 30 MINUTES (PLUS STANDING TIME) **COOKING TIME** 45 MINUTES (PLUS COOLING TIME)

Salmon roe, also referred to as red caviar, makes a wonderful hors d'oeuvre. Sold fresh, it is extremely perishable and should be consumed in about three days. Always keep, covered, under refrigeration.

3 small leeks (600g), sliced thinly
2 teaspoons salt
24 oysters, on the half shell (600g)
50g butter
¼ cup (60ml) water
2 tablespoons salmon roe

1 Combine leek and salt in sieve over medium bowl; stand 1 hour.
2 Meanwhile, remove oysters from shells; wash shells, dry thoroughly, reserve. Refrigerate oysters until required.
3 Rinse leek under cold water; drain. Pat dry with absorbent paper.
4 Melt butter in medium frying pan; cook leek with the water, uncovered, stirring occasionally, over low heat about 45 minutes or until leek breaks down and is almost pulpy. Cool 10 minutes.
5 Divide shells among serving plates; divide leek confit among shells. Place one oyster on leek mixture; top with roe.

serves 4
per serving 12.6g fat; 701kJ (167 cal)

tomato tarte tatins with crème fraîche sauce

PREPARATION TIME 40 MINUTES **COOKING TIME** 30 MINUTES

The original was a caramelised apple dessert tart named after the "demoiselles Tatin", two French sisters who created it in the late 1800s. Our version moves the tart up a course or two to star at the start of a meal. Shallots, also called french shallots, golden shallots or eschalots, are small, elongated members of the onion family that grow in clusters, similar to garlic.

9 small firm tomatoes (800g), peeled, quartered
30g butter
1 clove garlic, crushed
1 tablespoon brown sugar
2 tablespoons balsamic vinegar
1½ sheets ready-rolled butter puff pastry
1 egg, beaten lightly
vegetable oil, for deep-frying
6 sprigs fresh baby basil

CREME FRAICHE SAUCE
20g butter
2 shallots (50g), chopped finely
1 cup (240g) crème fraîche
⅓ cup (80ml) water

1 Preheat oven to moderately hot.
2 Discard pulp and seeds from tomato quarters; gently flatten flesh.
3 Melt butter in large frying pan; cook garlic, stirring, over low heat, until fragrant. Add sugar and vinegar; cook, stirring, until sugar dissolves. Place tomato in pan, in single layer; cook, covered, turning once, about 5 minutes or until tomato softens.
4 Oil six 1-cup (250ml) metal pie dishes; cut six 11cm rounds from pastry sheets. Divide tomato among dishes; top each with one pastry round, pressing down gently. Brush pastry with egg; bake, uncovered, in moderately hot oven about 15 minutes or until pastry is browned lightly and puffed.
5 Meanwhile, heat oil in small saucepan; using metal tongs, place thoroughly dry basil sprigs, one at a time, in pan. Deep-fry about 3 seconds or until basil is crisp. Drain on absorbent paper.
6 Make crème fraîche sauce.
7 Divide sauce among serving plates; turn tarts onto sauce, top with basil.

CREME FRAICHE SAUCE Melt butter in small saucepan; cook shallot, stirring, about 3 minutes or until softened. Add crème fraîche; cook, stirring, over low heat, until heated through. Stir in the water.

serves 6
per serving 33.4g fat; 1697kJ (405 cal)

TIP Take care when deep-frying the basil sprigs as the hot oil is likely to splatter.

Discard pulp and seeds from tomato quarters then flatten.

Cook tomato, in single layer, turning once, until soft.

Divide tomato among dishes then top each with pastry round.

light dishes and lunches

cheese-filled zucchini flowers with tomato basil sauce

PREPARATION TIME 40 MINUTES **COOKING TIME** 20 MINUTES

Green peppercorn cream cheese is a mild processed blend and makes the perfect stuffing for these delicate zucchini flowers. It can be found in the dairy section of supermarkets and in specialty cheese stores.

200g green peppercorn cream cheese, softened
1 tablespoon finely chopped fresh chives
¼ cup (15g) fresh breadcrumbs
16 baby zucchini with flowers attached (320g)
2 tablespoons olive oil

TOMATO BASIL SAUCE
1 tablespoon olive oil
1 small brown onion (80g), chopped finely
1 clove garlic, crushed
400g can diced tomatoes
1 tablespoon finely shredded fresh basil

1 Combine cheese, chives and breadcrumbs in small bowl. Discard stamens from zucchini flowers; fill flowers with cheese mixture, twist petal tops to enclose filling.
2 Make tomato basil sauce.
3 Meanwhile, heat oil in large frying pan; cook zucchini flowers, covered, about 5 minutes or until baby zucchini are tender, turning occasionally.
4 Remove zucchini carefully from dish to serving plates; serve with sauce.

TOMATO BASIL SAUCE Heat oil in medium frying pan; cook onion and garlic, stirring, until onion softens. Stir in undrained tomatoes; bring to a boil. Reduce heat; simmer, uncovered, about 20 minutes or until sauce thickens. Remove from heat; stir in basil.

serves 4
per serving 30.8g fat; 1399kJ (334 cal)

TIP Substitute any soft cheese, such as ricotta or neufchâtel, for the green peppercorn cheese, if you prefer.

goat cheese soufflé with creamed spinach sauce

PREPARATION TIME 15 MINUTES **COOKING TIME** 25 MINUTES (PLUS COOLING TIME)

Goat cheese, with its strong earthy taste, is available in both soft and firm textures, in various shapes and sizes, and often rolled in ash or herbs.

cooking-oil spray
¼ cup (25g) packaged
  breadcrumbs
30g butter
2 tablespoons plain flour
1 cup (250ml) milk
4 eggs, separated
¼ teaspoon cayenne pepper
150g firm goat cheese,
  crumbled

CREAMED SPINACH SAUCE
180g baby spinach leaves
⅔ cup (160ml) cream, warmed

1 Preheat oven to moderately hot. Spray six 1-cup (250ml) soufflé dishes with cooking-oil spray, sprinkle with breadcrumbs; place on oven tray.
2 Melt butter in small saucepan, add flour; cook, stirring, until mixture bubbles and thickens. Gradually add milk; stir until mixture boils and thickens. Transfer to large bowl; stir in egg yolks, pepper and cheese; cool 5 minutes.
3 Beat egg whites in small bowl with electric mixer until soft peaks form; gently fold whites, in two batches, into cheese mixture.
4 Divide mixture among prepared dishes. Bake, uncovered, in moderately hot oven about 15 minutes or until soufflés are puffed and browned lightly.
5 Meanwhile, make creamed spinach sauce.
6 Serve soufflés with sauce.

CREAMED SPINACH SAUCE Boil, steam or microwave spinach until just wilted; drain. Using hand, squeeze out excess liquid. Blend or process spinach until almost smooth. With motor operating, gradually add cream; process until smooth.

serves 6
per serving 24.4g fat; 1247kJ (298 cal)

terrine de campagne

PREPARATION TIME 20 MINUTES **COOKING TIME** 2 HOURS (PLUS REFRIGERATION TIME)

"Country-style terrine" is the literal meaning of this classic dish as it is chunky and rustic. Juniper berries, the dried fruit from the evergreen tree of the same name, can be found in specialty spice stores and better delicatessens.

350g chicken thigh fillets,
    chopped coarsely
400g boned pork belly, rind
    removed, chopped coarsely
300g piece calves liver,
    trimmed, chopped coarsely
3 bacon rashers (210g), rind
    removed, chopped coarsely
3 cloves garlic, crushed
2 teaspoons finely chopped
    fresh thyme
10 juniper berries, crushed
2 tablespoons port
¼ cup (60ml) dry white wine
1 egg
¼ cup (35g) toasted,
    shelled pistachios

1 Preheat oven to slow. Oil 1.5-litre (6-cup) ovenproof terrine dish.
2 Blend or process meats, separately, until coarsely minced; combine in large bowl with remaining ingredients.
3 Press meat mixture into prepared dish; cover with foil. Place terrine dish in baking dish; pour enough boiling water into baking dish to come halfway up side of terrine dish. Cook in slow oven 1 hour. Uncover; cook in slow oven about 1 hour or until cooked through.
4 Remove terrine dish from baking dish; cover terrine with baking paper. Weight with another dish filled with heavy cans; cool 10 minutes then refrigerate overnight.
5 Turn terrine onto serving plate; serve sliced terrine, at room temperature, with french bread and cornichons, if desired.

serves 6
per serving 27.6g fat; 1811kJ (433 cal)

Blend or process meats, separately, until coarsely minced.

Pour water into baking dish to come halfway up sides of terrine.

Cover terrine with baking paper then weight with heavy cans.

onion and anchovy tartlets

PREPARATION TIME 45 MINUTES **COOKING TIME** 35 MINUTES

1 tablespoon olive oil

60g butter

3 medium brown onions (450g), halved, sliced thinly

2 cloves garlic, crushed

1 bay leaf

3 sprigs fresh thyme

⅓ cup coarsely chopped fresh flat-leaf parsley

8 anchovy fillets, drained, chopped finely

2 tablespoons coarsely chopped seeded kalamata olives

¾ cup (110g) self-raising flour

¾ cup (110g) plain flour

¾ cup (180ml) buttermilk

1 Heat oil and half of the butter in large frying pan; cook onion, garlic, bay leaf and thyme, stirring occasionally, about 20 minutes or until onion caramelises. Discard bay leaf and thyme; stir in parsley, anchovy and olives.

2 Meanwhile, blend or process flours and remaining butter until mixture resembles fine breadcrumbs. Add buttermilk; process until ingredients just come together. Knead dough on lightly floured surface until smooth.

3 Preheat oven to moderately hot. Oil two oven trays.

4 Divide dough into six pieces; roll each piece of dough on floured surface into 14cm square. Fold edges over to form 1cm border.

5 Place squares on prepared trays; place rounded tablespoons of the onion mixture on each square. Bake, uncovered, in moderately hot oven about 15 minutes or until pastry browns lightly.

serves 6

per serving 12.9g fat; 1184kJ (283 cal)

potted pork with witlof and cornichons

PREPARATION TIME 30 MINUTES **COOKING TIME** 2 HOURS 30 MINUTES

Served as a light meal, potted meat, fish or poultry may also be accompanied with a basket of baguette slices and a glass of chilled, sweet white wine, as well as the cornichons and witlof as shown here.

¼ cup (60ml) water
1kg boned pork belly, rind removed, diced into 5cm pieces
3 bay leaves
2 cloves garlic, chopped coarsely
¼ cup (60ml) dry white wine
2 teaspoons salt
1 teaspoon ground black pepper
1 small red onion (100g), chopped finely
1 tablespoon finely chopped fresh flat-leaf parsley
⅔ cup (120g) drained cornichons
6 witlof (750g), trimmed, leaves separated

1 Preheat oven to slow.
2 Combine the water, pork, bay leaves, garlic, wine, salt and pepper in large shallow baking dish. Cook, covered, in slow oven about 2½ hours or until pork is very tender.
3 Discard bay leaves; using two forks, shred pork finely in dish with pan juices. Stir in onion and parsley. Serve pork with cornichons and witlof.

serves 8
per serving 38.6g fat; 1912kJ (457 cal)

Using two forks, shred pork finely while still in dish with pan juices.

veal sweetbreads with duxelles and herb salad

PREPARATION TIME 45 MINUTES (PLUS REFRIGERATION TIME) **COOKING TIME** 20 MINUTES (PLUS COOLING TIME)

Duxelles, a classic French mixture generally used in sauces, pâtés and terrines, stuffings and soup bases, is made of finely chopped mushrooms and various herbs sautéed in butter with shallots or green onions. Here, we've served it as a flavourful accompaniment to punctuate the mild creaminess of the sweetbreads.

500g veal sweetbreads
¼ cup (35g) plain flour
1 teaspoon salt
½ teaspoon freshly ground
   black pepper
¼ cup (60ml) olive oil
1 cup loosely packed fresh
   flat-leaf parsley leaves
1 cup loosely packed
   fresh basil leaves
1 cup loosely packed
   fresh chervil leaves
¾ cup coarsely chopped
   fresh chives
2 tablespoons olive oil, extra
2 tablespoons red wine vinegar

DUXELLES
40g butter
400g swiss brown mushrooms,
   chopped finely
8 shallots (200g),
   chopped finely
¼ cup (60ml) port
⅓ cup (80ml) beef stock
2 tablespoons finely chopped
   fresh flat-leaf parsley

1 Place sweetbreads in medium bowl, cover with cold water; refrigerate 4 hours, changing water once an hour, until sweetbreads whiten and water is clear. Cook sweetbreads, uncovered, in medium saucepan of boiling water 5 minutes; drain. Cool 10 minutes. Remove outer membranes then slice sweetbreads thickly.

2 Meanwhile, make duxelles.

3 Coat sweetbreads in combined flour, salt and pepper; shake away excess flour. Heat oil in large frying pan; cook sweetbreads, in batches, about 5 minutes or until browned lightly and cooked as desired.

4 Meanwhile, combine herbs in large bowl with extra oil and vinegar; toss gently to combine.

5 Serve sweetbreads with duxelles and herb salad.

DUXELLES Heat butter in large frying pan; cook mushrooms and shallot, stirring, until shallot softens. Add port and stock; bring to a boil. Reduce heat; simmer, uncovered, about 15 minutes or until liquid is evaporated. Remove from heat; stir in parsley.

serves 4
per serving 53.1g fat; 2902kJ (693 cal)

Sweetbreads should be soaked in cold water before being cooked.

Remove the outer membranes then slice sweetbreads thickly.

herb-crumbed brains with celeriac remoulade

PREPARATION TIME 30 MINUTES (PLUS REFRIGERATION TIME)
COOKING TIME 20 MINUTES (PLUS COOLING TIME)

Celeriac remoulade is something of a French-bistro-like spin on coleslaw, with the classic mayonnaise and cabbage combo given a bit more "oomph" by the addition of capers, gherkins and anchovies to the coarsely grated, piquant-tasting celeriac.

6 sets lamb brains (600g)
1 litre (4 cups) water
1 tablespoon lemon juice
1 teaspoon salt
1 cup (70g) stale breadcrumbs
2 green onions, chopped finely
1 tablespoon finely chopped
  fresh flat-leaf parsley
2 tablespoons finely chopped
  fresh tarragon
½ teaspoon cracked
  black pepper
¼ cup (35g) plain flour
1 egg, beaten lightly
2 tablespoons milk
vegetable oil, for deep-frying

CELERIAC REMOULADE
½ cup (150g) mayonnaise
200g celeriac, grated coarsely
2 anchovy fillets, drained,
  chopped finely
2 tablespoons drained capers,
  rinsed, chopped finely
1 tablespoon finely chopped
  fresh flat-leaf parsley
1 tablespoon lemon juice

1 Remove brain stem by pulling away gently with fingers; divide each set of brains into two lobes. Place in large bowl, cover with cold water; refrigerate, covered, 2 hours. Drain.

2 Combine brains in medium saucepan with the water, juice and salt; bring to a boil. Reduce heat; simmer, uncovered, 5 minutes. Drain; cool 10 minutes.

3 Meanwhile, make celeriac remoulade.

4 Combine breadcrumbs, onion, herbs and pepper in large bowl. Coat brains in flour; shake away excess. Dip brains in combined egg and milk then coat in breadcrumb mixture.

5 Heat oil in large saucepan; deep-fry brains, in batches, until browned lightly. Drain on absorbent paper. Serve brains hot with celeriac remoulade and assorted salad greens, if desired.

CELERIAC REMOULADE Combine ingredients in medium bowl.

serves 4
per serving 56.9g fat; 2924kJ (699 cal)

Remove brain stem by pulling it away gently with your fingers.

Divide each set of brains into two lobes then place in bowl of water.

roast bacon-wrapped quail with muscat sauce

PREPARATION TIME 15 MINUTES **COOKING TIME** 30 MINUTES

Muscat is a sweet, aromatic dessert wine, possessing an almost musty flavour. It is made from the fully matured muscatel grape.

4 quails (780g)
1 lemon
20g butter
4 bacon rashers (280g), rind removed
⅓ cup (80ml) muscat
250g green beans
½ cup (125ml) chicken stock
150g fresh muscatel grapes, halved

1 Preheat oven to moderately hot.
2 Discard necks from quails. Wash quails under cold water; pat dry with absorbent paper.
3 Halve lemon; cut one lemon half into four wedges. Place one lemon wedge and a quarter of the butter inside each quail. Tuck legs along body, wrapping tightly with bacon rasher to hold legs in place.
4 Place quails in medium flameproof casserole dish; drizzle with one tablespoon of the muscat and juice of remaining lemon half. Roast, uncovered, in moderately hot oven about 25 minutes or until quails are browned and cooked through. Remove quails from dish; cover to keep warm.
5 Meanwhile, boil, steam or microwave beans until tender; drain. Cover to keep warm.
6 Return dish with pan liquid to heat, add remaining muscat and stock; stir until sauce boils and reduces to about ½ cup. Add grapes; stir until heated though. Serve quail on beans topped with muscat sauce.

Tuck legs alongside body; wrap tightly with bacon rasher.

serves 4
per serving 21.6g fat; 1515kJ (362 cal)

salade composé

PREPARATION TIME 15 MINUTES **COOKING TIME** 20 MINUTES

Literally meaning "composed salad", the ingredients in this dish are layered on top of each other, rather than being tossed together, and the dressing is drizzled over the top.

1 small french bread stick
2 cloves garlic, crushed
¼ cup (60ml) olive oil
6 bacon rashers (420g), rind removed, sliced thickly
150g mesclun
6 medium egg tomatoes (450g), sliced thinly
4 hard-boiled eggs, halved lengthways

RED WINE VINAIGRETTE
¼ cup (60ml) red wine vinegar
3 teaspoons dijon mustard
⅓ cup (80ml) extra virgin olive oil

1 Preheat grill.
2 Cut bread into 1cm slices. Brush both sides with combined garlic and oil; toast under preheated grill.
3 Cook bacon in large frying pan until crisp; drain on absorbent paper.
4 Meanwhile, make red wine vinaigrette.
5 Layer bread and bacon in large bowl with mesclun and tomato, top with egg; drizzle with vinaigrette.

RED WINE VINAIGRETTE Place ingredients in screw-top jar; shake well.

serves 4
per serving 46g fat; 2413kJ (577 cal)

spinach salad with mushrooms, poached egg and anchovy dressing

PREPARATION TIME 20 MINUTES **COOKING TIME** 10 MINUTES

40g butter

2 flat mushrooms (200g), sliced thickly

100g swiss brown mushrooms, sliced thickly

100g shiitake mushrooms, sliced thickly

4 eggs

270g char-grilled capsicum in oil, drained, sliced thinly

300g baby spinach leaves

ANCHOVY DRESSING

2 tablespoons coarsely chopped fresh sage

1 tablespoon drained capers, rinsed

6 anchovy fillets, drained

2 tablespoons balsamic vinegar

¼ cup (60ml) olive oil

2 tablespoons water

1 Make anchovy dressing.

2 Melt butter in large frying pan; cook mushrooms, stirring, until tender. Place in large bowl; cover to keep warm.

3 Half-fill a large shallow frying pan with water; bring to a boil. Break eggs into cup, one at a time, then slide into pan. When all eggs are in pan, allow water to return to a boil. Cover pan, turn off heat; stand about 4 minutes or until a light film of egg white sets over yolks. Remove eggs, one at a time, using slotted spoon, and place on absorbent-paper-lined saucer to blot up poaching liquid.

4 Add capsicum and half of the dressing to mushroom mixture in large bowl; toss gently to combine.

5 Divide spinach among serving plates; top with mushroom mixture and egg, drizzle with remaining dressing.

ANCHOVY DRESSING Blend or process ingredients until combined.

serves 4

per serving 32.5g fat; 1949kJ (466 cal)

lentil and goat cheese salad

PREPARATION TIME 40 MINUTES **COOKING TIME** 30 MINUTES

Puy lentils, a superior variety of small green lentils originally sourced from
the town of Puy in the Auvergne region in central France, are excellent in
salads because they retain a slight firmness after being cooked.

1 medium red capsicum (200g),
  sliced thickly
2 tablespoons extra virgin
  olive oil
½ cup (110g) puy lentils,
  rinsed, drained
1 medium brown onion (150g),
  halved
1 bay leaf
16 sprigs fresh thyme
300g piece firm goat cheese
2 tablespoons packaged
  breadcrumbs
2 teaspoons finely grated
  lemon rind
1 tablespoon coarsely chopped
  fresh flat-leaf parsley
250g cherry tomatoes, halved
100g mesclun

VINAIGRETTE
1 tablespoon red wine vinegar
2 tablespoons extra virgin
  olive oil
1 teaspoon dijon mustard
1 teaspoon sugar

1 Preheat oven to hot.
2 Combine capsicum and half of the oil in large shallow baking dish; toss
   to coat capsicum. Roast, uncovered, in hot oven about 15 minutes or
   until capsicum just softens.
3 Meanwhile, combine lentils, onion, bay leaf and thyme in medium
   saucepan, cover with water; bring to a boil. Reduce heat; simmer,
   covered, about 20 minutes or until lentils just tender. Drain; discard
   onion, bay leaf and thyme.
4 Meanwhile, make vinaigrette.
5 Cut cheese into 16 pieces; coat cheese in breadcrumbs. Heat
   remaining oil in medium frying pan; cook cheese, uncovered, about
   5 minutes or until cheese is browned lightly all over and starting to melt.
6 Meanwhile, combine lentils in medium bowl with rind, parsley, tomato
   and two-thirds of the vinaigrette. Divide lentils among serving plates; top
   with capsicum, mesclun then cheese, drizzle with remaining vinaigrette.

VINAIGRETTE Place ingredients in screw-top jar; shake well.

serves 4
per serving 31g fat; 1779kJ (425 cal)

mains

châteaubriand

PREPARATION TIME 45 MINUTES **COOKING TIME** 50 MINUTES

Named after the 19th-century author François Châteaubriand, this special-occasion dish has become synonymous with the cut of beef used in its presentation.

1kg medium potatoes
40g unsalted butter
¼ cup (60ml) olive oil
2 tablespoons finely chopped
  fresh garlic chives
750g piece beef eye fillet
400g baby vine-ripened
  truss tomatoes
400g baby carrots, trimmed
350g broccolini
250g yellow patty-pan squash

BEARNAISE SAUCE

⅓ cup (80ml) white wine vinegar
½ teaspoon black peppercorns
2 green onions, chopped finely
3 egg yolks
150g unsalted butter, melted
2 teaspoons finely chopped
  fresh tarragon

MUSHROOM SAUCE

1 medium brown onion (150g),
  chopped finely
150g button mushrooms,
  quartered
150g oyster mushrooms,
  sliced thickly
½ cup (125ml) beef stock
¼ cup (60ml) dry red wine
¼ cup (60ml) cream

1 Preheat oven to hot.
2 Make béarnaise sauce.
3 Cut potatoes into 1cm slices. Heat butter and half of the oil in large non-stick frying pan; cook potato, uncovered, turning occasionally, until browned lightly. Reduce heat; cook potato, covered, turning occasionally, about 15 minutes or until tender. Stir in chives.
4 Meanwhile, heat remaining oil in medium flameproof casserole dish; cook beef, uncovered, until browned all over. Place dish in oven; roast beef, uncovered, in hot oven 10 minutes. Add tomatoes to dish; roast, uncovered, about 10 minutes or until beef is cooked as desired and tomatoes are soft. Remove beef and tomatoes from dish; cover to keep warm.
5 Make mushroom sauce, using dish with beef juices.
6 Boil, steam or microwave carrots, broccolini and squash, separately, until just tender; drain. Serve beef with potato and vegetables on large serving platter accompanied with both sauces.

BEARNAISE SAUCE Combine vinegar, peppercorns and onion in small saucepan; bring to a boil. Reduce heat; simmer, uncovered, about 5 minutes or until liquid has reduced by half. Strain over medium heatproof bowl; discard peppercorns and onion. Whisk yolks into liquid in bowl until combined. Set bowl over medium saucepan of simmering water; gradually whisk in melted butter in thin, steady stream until mixture thickens slightly. Remove from heat; stir in tarragon. Cover to keep warm.

MUSHROOM SAUCE Place same flameproof casserole dish with beef juices over medium heat, add onion and mushrooms; cook, stirring, until onion softens. Add stock, wine and cream; bring to a boil. Reduce heat; simmer, uncovered, stirring, about 10 minutes or until sauce thickens slightly and mushrooms are tender. Cover to keep warm.

serves 6
per serving 49.7g fat; 3066kJ (732 cal)

cassoulet

PREPARATION TIME 40 MINUTES (PLUS STANDING TIME) **COOKING TIME** 2 HOURS 10 MINUTES

Our version of this classic takes its lead from the traditional versions of Languedoc and Castelnaudary, but we've given it an update to make it a simpler, quicker and healthier dish. Haricot, great northern, cannellini or navy beans can be used in this recipe.

1½ cups (300g) dried
  white beans
300g boned pork belly, rind
  removed, sliced thinly
150g piece streaky bacon,
  rind removed, diced into
  1cm pieces
800g piece boned lamb
  shoulder, diced into
  3cm pieces
1 large brown onion (200g),
  chopped finely
1 small leek (200g), sliced thinly
2 cloves garlic, crushed
3 sprigs fresh thyme
400g can crushed tomatoes
2 bay leaves
1 cup (250ml) water
1 cup (250ml) chicken stock
2 cups (140g) stale breadcrumbs
⅓ cup coarsely chopped
  fresh flat-leaf parsley

1 Place beans in medium bowl, cover with water; soak overnight, drain. Rinse under cold water; drain. Place beans in medium saucepan of boiling water; bring to a boil. Reduce heat; simmer, covered, about 15 minutes or until beans are just tender. Drain.

2 Preheat oven to moderately slow.

3 Cook pork in large flameproof casserole dish over heat, pressing down with back of spoon on pork until browned all over; remove from dish. Cook bacon in same pan, stirring, until crisp; remove from dish. Cook lamb, in batches, in same pan, until browned all over.

4 Cook onion, leek and garlic in same dish, stirring, until onion softens. Add thyme, undrained tomatoes, bay leaves, the water, stock, beans and meat; bring to a boil. Cover; cook in moderately slow oven 45 minutes. Remove from oven; sprinkle with combined breadcrumbs and parsley. Return to oven; cook, uncovered, about 45 minutes or until liquid is nearly absorbed and beans are tender.

serves 6
per serving 27.6g fat; 2154kJ (514 cal)

coq à la bière

PREPARATION TIME 30 MINUTES **COOKING TIME** 1 HOUR 50 MINUTES

Coq à la bière is a specialty of the beer-producing region of Alsace, but this recipe uses a pale ale instead of the traditional dark brew... and the result is a lighter, more delicately flavoured sauce that suits the chicken perfectly. Shallots, also called french shallots, golden shallots or eschalots, are small, elongated, brown-skinned members of the onion family that grow in tight clusters similar to garlic.

1.4kg chicken
¼ cup (35g) plain flour
20g butter
2 large carrots (360g)
1 tablespoon olive oil
6 shallots (150g), peeled
2 tablespoons brandy
1½ cups (375ml) pale ale
1 cup (250ml) chicken stock
1 bay leaf
2 sprigs fresh thyme
2 sprigs fresh flat-leaf parsley
20g butter, extra
200g mushrooms
½ cup (125ml) cream

1 Halve chicken lengthways; cut halves crossways through the centre. Separate breasts from wings; separate thighs from legs.
2 Coat chicken pieces in flour; shake off excess. Melt butter in large saucepan; cook chicken, in batches, until browned all over.
3 Meanwhile, cut carrots into 5cm lengths; cut lengths in half lengthways then cut halves thickly into strips.
4 Heat oil in same cleaned pan; cook shallots, stirring occasionally, about 5 minutes or until browned lightly. Add carrot; cook, stirring, 5 minutes. Add brandy; cook, stirring, until liquid evaporates. Add chicken, ale, stock and herbs; bring to a boil. Reduce heat; simmer, uncovered, 1¼ hours.
5 Melt extra butter in medium frying pan; cook mushrooms, stirring, until just tender. Add mushrooms and cream to chicken; cook, covered, 15 minutes. Serve coq à la bière with mashed potatoes, if desired.

serves 4
per serving 51.2g fat; 3067kJ (733 cal)

pot au feu with stuffed cabbage rolls

PREPARATION TIME 45 MINUTES **COOKING TIME** 1 HOUR 45 MINUTES

The literal translation of "pot on the fire" refers to the way this old standard was originally cooked, in a huge cast-iron pot directly in the fireplace. Any combination of vegetables and meat can be used, and the French versions are as numerous as there are regions of the country.

2 veal shanks (1.5kg)
2 large carrots (360g),
    chopped coarsely
1 medium leek (350g),
    chopped coarsely
2 small turnips (300g),
    chopped coarsely
6 baby onions (150g)
1 bay leaf
3 cups (750ml) chicken stock
1 litre (4 cups) water
1 small savoy cabbage (1.2kg)
250g pork mince
250g chicken mince
1 egg
1 small brown onion (80g),
    chopped finely
½ cup (50g) packaged
    breadcrumbs

1 Place veal, carrot, leek, turnip, whole onions, bay leaf, stock and the water in large saucepan; bring to a boil. Reduce heat; simmer, uncovered, about 1½ hours or until veal is tender. Remove veal; when cool enough to handle, remove meat from bones and chop it coarsely.

2 Remove 12 large leaves from cabbage; cook, uncovered, in batches, in large saucepan of boiling water 3 minutes. Drain leaves on absorbent paper. Finely chop enough of the remaining cabbage to make ⅓ cup; reserve remaining cabbage for another use.

3 Meanwhile, using hand combine pork, chicken, egg, onion, breadcrumbs and chopped cabbage in large bowl; divide mixture among cabbage leaves. Roll leaves to enclose filling, secure with toothpicks.

4 Return veal meat to vegetable mixture in pan, add cabbage rolls; bring to a boil. Reduce heat; simmer, uncovered, about 10 minutes or until cabbage rolls are cooked through. Divide cabbage rolls among serving bowls; ladle soup over top.

serves 6
per serving 12.3g fat; 1766kJ (422 cal)

TIP When peeling turnips, make sure you remove all the bitter outer layer.

Roll leaves to enclose filling, then secure each roll with a toothpick.

pork cutlet with stuffed apple and peppercorn cider sauce

PREPARATION TIME 20 MINUTES **COOKING TIME** 1 HOUR

40g butter
1 small brown onion (80g), chopped finely
1 clove garlic, crushed
1 bacon rasher (70g), rind removed, chopped finely
¼ cup (15g) stale breadcrumbs
2 seeded prunes (20g), chopped finely
2 tablespoons finely chopped fresh chives
2 large apples (400g)
10g butter, extra
4 pork cutlets (940g)
½ cup (125ml) sparkling apple cider
2 teaspoons drained green peppercorns, crushed
300ml cream

1 Preheat oven to moderate.

2 Melt butter in large frying pan; cook onion, garlic and bacon, stirring, until onion softens. Stir in breadcrumbs, prunes and half of the chives.

3 Core apples; pierce apples in several places with fork. Press breadcrumb mixture into apple centres; place in large deep flameproof baking dish. Melt extra butter; brush all over apples. Cook, uncovered, in moderate oven 30 minutes.

4 Meanwhile, lightly oil same cleaned pan; cook pork, uncovered, about 2 minutes each side or until browned. Place pork in same dish with apples; cover with foil. Cook in moderate oven with apples about 15 minutes or until pork is cooked as desired.

5 Remove pork and apples from dish; cover to keep warm. Stir cider and peppercorns into juices in dish; cook, stirring, 1 minute. Add cream; bring to a boil. Reduce heat; simmer, uncovered, until sauce thickens slightly. Stir in remaining chives. Halve apples; serve with pork, drizzle with sauce and serve with mash, if desired.

serves 4
per serving 41.9g fat; 2559kJ (611 cal)

pork belly and spicy sausage with braised lettuce

PREPARATION TIME 40 MINUTES (PLUS REFRIGERATION TIME) **COOKING TIME** 40 MINUTES

Merguez is a small, spicy sausage that originated in Tunisia, but was quickly claimed by cooks throughout North Africa and Spain. Traditionally made with lamb, and is easily recognised because of its chilli-red colour, merguez can be fried, grilled or roasted, and is most often eaten with couscous. It can be found in many butchers, delicatessens and sausage specialty shops.

4 merguez sausages (320g)
200g pork mince
1 teaspoon finely chopped
   fresh thyme
500g boned pork belly,
   rind removed
1 cup (220g) sugar
½ cup (125ml) apple juice
1¼ cup (310ml) chicken stock
20g butter
2 large butter lettuces (1kg),
   trimmed, shredded finely

1 Using sharp knife, slit sausage skins; discard skins. Combine sausage meat in medium bowl with pork mince and thyme. Roll mixture into sausage shape measuring about 5cm in diameter and 20cm in length. Wrap sausage tightly in baking paper then foil, twisting ends tightly to seal. Wrap sausage once again, this time in plastic wrap, twisting ends tightly; refrigerate 1 hour.

2 Meanwhile, cut pork belly, across grain, into 1cm slices; cut each slice in half. Cook pork in large non-stick frying pan about 10 minutes, pressing down with back of spoon until browned and crisp. Drain on absorbent paper.

3 Cook sausage in large saucepan of boiling water, covered, 30 minutes.

4 Meanwhile, combine sugar and apple juice in large heavy-based saucepan. Stir over heat, without boiling, until sugar dissolves; bring to a boil. Reduce heat; simmer, uncovered, without stirring, about 10 minutes or until mixture is browned lightly. Gradually add 1 cup of the stock, stirring until apple sauce is smooth.

5 Melt butter in large saucepan; cook lettuce, stirring, 5 minutes. Add remaining stock; cook, uncovered, until stock evaporates.

6 Reheat apple sauce until almost boiling; add pork, stir about 2 minutes or until pork is heated through.

7 Remove sausage from wrapping; cut into 12 slices. Divide lettuce mixture, sausage and pork among serving plates; drizzle with apple sauce.

serves 6
per serving 40.7g fat; 2807kJ (671 cal)

Using sharp knife, slit sausage skins; discard skins.

Wrap log tightly in baking paper then foil, twisting ends tightly.

Using sharp knife, cut pork belly across grain into 1cm slices.

veal medallions with sauce poivrade and potato gratin

PREPARATION TIME 30 MINUTES **COOKING TIME** 1 HOUR 20 MINUTES (PLUS STANDING TIME)

A sauce poivrade, made with vinegar, pepper and meat or pan juices, is the perfect sauce to go with these tender veal medallions. We used sebago potatoes for this recipe, but you can use any floury potato, such as nicola or lasoda, if you prefer.

2 veal fillets (1.2kg)
40g butter
2 shallots (50g), chopped finely
1 small carrot (70g),
    chopped finely
1 trimmed celery stalk (100g),
    chopped finely
1 clove garlic, crushed
2 tablespoons black
    peppercorns, crushed
1 tablespoon plain flour
2 tablespoons red wine vinegar
1 cup (250ml) dry red wine
2 cups (500ml) beef stock
2 tablespoons redcurrant jelly

POTATO GRATIN
1¾ cups (430ml) cream
¾ cup (180ml) milk
2 cloves garlic, crushed
1kg potatoes, cut into
    2mm slices
1 medium brown onion (150g),
    sliced thinly
2 tablespoons finely grated
    parmesan cheese

1 Make potato gratin.
2 Trim veal fillets; chop trimmings coarsely. Cut each fillet on the diagonal into nine slices; press with side of heavy knife or meat mallet to flatten.
3 Melt half of the butter in medium saucepan; cook veal trimmings with shallot, carrot, celery, garlic and pepper, stirring, until onion softens. Add flour; cook, stirring, until mixture bubbles and thickens. Add vinegar; cook, stirring, until absorbed. Gradually add wine and stock; stir until mixture boils and thickens. Reduce heat, simmer, uncovered, until sauce is reduced to about 1½ cups. Strain into small bowl; discard solids. Return sauce to same cleaned pan; whisk in jelly and remaining butter until sauce is smooth.
4 Meanwhile, cook veal in large lightly oiled frying pan, in batches, about 45 seconds each side or until cooked as desired. Divide potato gratin among serving plates; top with veal medallions, drizzled with sauce.

POTATO GRATIN Preheat oven to moderately hot. Combine cream, milk and garlic in small saucepan; bring to a boil. Combine potato with cream mixture in large bowl; layer half of the potato mixture in oiled deep 19cm-square cake pan. Layer with onion then layer with remaining potato, sprinkle with cheese. Cover with foil; cook in moderately hot oven 1 hour. Remove foil; cook in moderately hot oven about 20 minutes or until potato is tender and top lightly browned. Stand 20 minutes before cutting.

serves 6
per serving 37.2g fat; 2909kJ (695 cal)

TIPS Slice potatoes on a mandoline or V-slicer for consistent thickness. Crush peppercorns using a mortar and pestle.

veal shin on mushroom ragoût

PREPARATION TIME 15 MINUTES **COOKING TIME** 2 HOURS 15 MINUTES

Ragoût, derived from a French word loosely meaning "appetite stimulator", is a luscious, slowly cooked meat and vegetable stew.

40g butter
4 pieces veal shin (osso buco) (1kg)
2 cloves garlic, crushed
1 tablespoon fresh rosemary leaves
½ cup (125ml) port
1 cup (250ml) beef stock

MUSHROOM RAGOUT
40g butter
2 cloves garlic, crushed
1 large flat mushroom (100g), sliced thickly
200g swiss brown mushrooms, trimmed
200g shiitake mushrooms, sliced thickly
1 medium red capsicum (200g), sliced thickly
1 medium green capsicum (200g), sliced thickly
½ cup (125ml) beef stock
2 tablespoons port

1 Preheat oven to moderately slow.
2 Melt butter in medium flameproof casserole dish; cook veal, uncovered, until browned both sides. Add garlic, rosemary, port and stock; cook, covered, in moderately slow oven 2¼ hours.
3 Meanwhile, make mushroom ragoût.
4 Divide veal and ragoût among serving dishes; serve with soft polenta, if desired.

MUSHROOM RAGOUT Heat butter in large frying pan; cook garlic, mushrooms and capsicums, stirring, until vegetables are browned lightly and tender. Stir in stock and port; cook, covered, 30 minutes.

serves 4
per serving 21g fat; 1898kJ (453 cal)

seared calves liver with persillade and parsnip mash

PREPARATION TIME 15 MINUTES **COOKING TIME** 30 MINUTES

Persillade is a mixture of chopped garlic and parsley traditionally used either as a garnish or to flavour a sauce, as we have done here. The secret to tender calves liver is to make sure you slice it into paper-thin scallops and then quickly sear it – overcooking will toughen its delicate texture. Shallots, also called french shallots, golden shallots or eschalots, are small, elongated, brown-skinned members of the onion family that grow in tight clusters similar to garlic.

1kg parsnips, chopped coarsely
1 large potato (300g), chopped coarsely
3 cloves garlic
½ cup (125ml) cream
100g butter
250g asparagus, trimmed
400g piece calves liver, sliced thinly
1 shallot (25g), chopped finely
½ cup (125ml) chicken stock
1 tablespoon lemon juice
⅓ cup finely chopped fresh flat-leaf parsley

1 Boil, steam or microwave parsnip and potato, separately, until tender; drain. Crush 2 cloves of the garlic; mash in large bowl with parsnip, potato, cream and half of the butter. Cover to keep warm.

2 Boil, steam or microwave asparagus until just tender; drain. Cover to keep warm.

3 Pat liver dry with absorbent paper. Melt about 1 tablespoon of the remaining butter in large frying pan; cook liver quickly, in batches, over high heat until browned both sides and cooked as desired (do not overcook). Cover to keep warm.

4 To make persillade, heat remaining butter in same pan. Finely chop remaining clove of garlic; cook garlic and shallot, stirring, until shallot softens. Add stock and juice; bring to a boil, stirring. Remove from heat; stir in parsley. Serve sliced liver with parsnip mash and asparagus; top liver with persillade.

serves 4
per serving 41.3g fat; 2577kJ (616 cal)

TIP When peeling parsnips, make sure you remove all the bitter outer layer.

chicken liver salad with polenta croûtons

PREPARATION TIME 30 MINUTES (PLUS STANDING TIME) **COOKING TIME** 45 MINUTES (PLUS REFRIGERATION TIME)

2 cups (500ml) water

2 cups (500ml) chicken stock

1 cup (170g) polenta

20g butter

2 tablespoons finely grated
   parmesan cheese

cooking-oil spray

1kg chicken livers, trimmed

1 cup (250ml) milk

½ cup (75g) plain flour

1 teaspoon salt

1 teaspoon cracked
   black pepper

¼ cup (60ml) olive oil

150g baby spinach leaves

1 small red onion (100g),
   sliced thinly

60g firm blue cheese

SHALLOT DRESSING

3 shallots (75g), chopped finely

2 tablespoons red wine vinegar

2 tablespoons olive oil

1 Lightly oil 19cm x 29cm slice pan.

2 Place the water and stock in large saucepan; bring to a boil. Gradually add polenta, stirring constantly. Reduce heat; cook, stirring, about 10 minutes or until polenta thickens. Stir in butter and parmesan then spread into prepared pan; cool 10 minutes. Cover; refrigerate about 3 hours or until firm. Cut into 2cm-square croûtons.

3 Meanwhile, make shallot dressing.

4 Preheat oven to moderate.

5 Oil two oven trays; place polenta croûtons, in single layer, on prepared trays. Spray croûtons with cooking-oil spray; bake, uncovered, in moderate oven about 30 minutes or until browned lightly and crisp.

6 Meanwhile, soak livers in milk in medium bowl 30 minutes. Separate livers into halves by cutting lobes apart. Coat liver in combined flour, salt and pepper; shake off excess. Heat oil in large frying pan; cook liver, over high heat, about 5 minutes or until browned and cooked as desired (do not overcook). Drain on absorbent paper.

7 Place spinach, onion, croûtons, liver and dressing in large bowl; toss gently to combine. Serve salad sprinkled with blue cheese.

SHALLOT DRESSING Place ingredients in screw-top jar; shake well.

serves 6
per serving 31.5g fat; 2366kJ (565 cal)

Separate chicken livers into halves by cutting lobes apart.

fillet steaks with caramelised shallots and creamy mashed potatoes

PREPARATION TIME 20 MINUTES **COOKING TIME** 40 MINUTES

We used lasoda potatoes for this recipe, but you can use any floury potato, such as nicola or sebago, if you prefer.

1kg potatoes, chopped coarsely
50g butter, chopped
½ cup (125ml) cream
16 shallots (400g)
3 green onions
2 teaspoons olive oil
20g butter, extra
1 teaspoon brown sugar
⅓ cup (80ml) dry red wine
2 cups (500ml) beef stock
4 x 150g beef fillet steaks

1 Boil, steam or microwave potato until tender; drain. Push potato through sieve into large bowl, add butter and cream; mash. Cover to keep warm.

2 Meanwhile, peel shallots leaving roots intact; cut green onions into 8cm lengths. Heat oil and extra butter in medium frying pan; cook shallots and green onion, stirring, until shallots are browned lightly and softened.

3 Remove green onion from pan; reserve. Add sugar to pan; cook over low heat, stirring, about 10 minutes or until shallots are caramelised.

4 Add wine and stock to pan; bring to a boil. Reduce heat; simmer, uncovered, about 10 minutes or until mixture thickens slightly. Return green onion to pan; simmer, uncovered, 2 minutes.

5 Meanwhile, cook beef on heated oiled grill plate (or grill or barbecue) until browned both sides and cooked as desired. Divide beef, mash and shallot mixture among serving plates; drizzle with any remaining shallot sauce.

serves 4
per serving 34.4g fat; 2619kJ (626 cal)

beef sirloin with herb butter and pommes frites

PREPARATION TIME 20 MINUTES (PLUS STANDING TIME) **COOKING TIME** 30 MINUTES

Our look at a French bistro's bifstek frites cooks a tender piece of beef to individual perfection and accompanies it with freshly made fries and a generous dab of basil-parsley butter. The potatoes have been twice-cooked to guarantee their crispness. We used sirloin with the bone in, but rib eye, fillet from the rump or eye fillet steaks are all suitable for this recipe. We used russet burbank potatoes in this recipe, but you can use any floury potato, such as bintje or sebago, if you prefer.

3 large potatoes (900g)
1½ tablespoons cracked
  black pepper
2 teaspoons salt
4 x 250g beef sirloin steaks
peanut oil, for deep-frying
1 tablespoon olive oil

HERBED BUTTER

1 clove garlic
60g butter, softened
2 tablespoons finely chopped
  fresh basil
2 tablespoons finely chopped
  fresh flat-leaf parsley

1 Cut peeled potatoes into 5mm slices; cut each slice into 5mm strips. Place potato in large bowl, cover with water; stand 1 hour. Drain; pat dry with absorbent paper.

2 Meanwhile, make herbed butter.

3 Combine pepper and salt on oven tray; press both sides of beef into pepper and salt mixture. Rest beef on oven tray while making frites.

4 Heat peanut oil in wok or large saucepan; cook potato, in batches, about 3 minutes or until just tender, but not browned. Drain on absorbent paper.

5 Meanwhile, heat olive oil in large frying pan; cook beef until browned both sides and cooked as desired. Cover; stand 5 minutes.

6 Reheat oil in wok; cook potato, in batches, until browned lightly and crisp. Drain frites on absorbent paper.

7 Divide beef among serving plates; top with herbed butter, serve with pommes frites.

HERBED BUTTER Place ingredients in small bowl, beat until combined. Place on piece of plastic wrap, wrap tightly, shape into rectangle; refrigerate until just firm.

serves 4
per serving 51.6g fat; 3417kJ (816 cal)

beef bourguignon pies with chips

PREPARATION TIME 30 MINUTES **COOKING TIME** 2 HOURS

We used frozen potato chips labelled on the package as "crunchy" – which they certainly are (and they suit these rich and saucy pies to a T!).

12 pickling onions (480g)
6 bacon rashers (420g), rind
    removed, sliced thinly
2 tablespoons olive oil
400g mushrooms
1kg gravy beef, trimmed,
    cut into 2cm pieces
¼ cup (35g) plain flour
1 tablespoon tomato paste
2 teaspoons fresh thyme leaves
1 cup (250ml) dry red wine
2 cups (500ml) beef stock
750g packet frozen
    potato chips
2 sheets ready-rolled
    butter puff pastry
cooking-oil spray
½ cup finely chopped
    fresh flat-leaf parsley

1 Peel onions, leaving roots intact; halve lengthways.
2 Cook bacon in heated large heavy-based saucepan, stirring, until crisp; drain on absorbent paper. Reheat same pan; cook onion, stirring, until browned all over, remove from pan. Heat 2 teaspoons of the oil in same pan; cook mushrooms, stirring, until just browned, remove from pan.
3 Coat beef in flour; shake off excess. Heat remaining oil in same pan; cook beef, in batches, until browned all over. Add bacon and onion with tomato paste and thyme; cook, stirring, 2 minutes. Add wine and stock; bring to a boil. Reduce heat; simmer, covered, 1 hour. Add mushrooms; simmer, uncovered, about 40 minutes or until beef is tender, stirring occasionally.
4 Meanwhile, preheat oven to hot. Cook chips according to directions on packet.
5 Place pastry sheets on board; using 1¼-cup (310ml) ovenproof dish, cut lid for one pie by tracing around upper-rim of dish with tip of sharp knife. Repeat process until you have six lids. Place lids on oiled oven tray, spray with cooking-oil spray; bake, uncovered, in hot oven during last 4 minutes of chip cooking-time or until lids are browned lightly.
6 Meanwhile, stir parsley into beef bourguignon then divide among six 1¼-cup (310ml) ovenproof dishes; top each with pastry lid. Serve pies with hot chips.

serves 6
per serving 45.6g fat; 4228kJ (1010 cal)

Cut lids for pies by tracing around dish with tip of sharp knife.

duck breasts with
fig sauce and spinach risoni

PREPARATION TIME 20 MINUTES **COOKING TIME** 25 MINUTES

Risoni, like orzo, is a very small rice-shaped pasta. It is great added to soups, baked in a casserole or as a side dish when served with a main course.

4 duck breast fillets (600g)
4 sprigs fresh rosemary
4 bay leaves
200g risoni
20g butter
200g baby spinach leaves, trimmed
1 small brown onion (80g), chopped finely
6 dried figs (90g), quartered
1 cup (250ml) port
1 cup (250ml) chicken stock
20g butter, extra

1 Use fingers to make pocket between meat and fat of each duck breast; press 1 sprig rosemary and 1 bay leaf into each pocket. Prick duck skins with fork several times; cook duck, skin-side down, in heated large lightly oiled frying pan about 8 minutes or until browned and crisp. Turn duck; cook about 5 minutes or until cooked as desired. Remove from pan; cover to keep warm.

2 Cook pasta in large saucepan of boiling water, uncovered, until just tender; drain. Place pasta in large bowl with butter and spinach; toss gently to combine. Cover to keep warm.

3 Meanwhile, cook onion in same frying pan as duck, stirring, until soft. Add fig, port and stock; bring to a boil. Reduce heat; simmer, stirring, about 5 minutes or until sauce thickens. Add extra butter; whisk until sauce is combined. Slice duck thinly; serve with risoni and fig sauce.

serves 4
per serving 64.7g fat; 4087kJ (976 cal)

Use fingers to make a pocket between breast meat and fat.

slow-roasted duck with sour cherry, apple and walnut salad

PREPARATION TIME 40 MINUTES **COOKING TIME** 2 HOURS

680g jar morello cherries
½ cup (125ml) chicken stock
½ cup (125ml) port
1 cinnamon stick
3 whole cloves
1 clove garlic, crushed
4 duck marylands (1.2kg),
    excess fat removed
2 small green apples (260g)
1 cup (100g) toasted walnuts,
    chopped coarsely
3 green onions, sliced thinly
1 cup firmly packed fresh
    flat-leaf parsley leaves
2 tablespoons olive oil
1 tablespoon lemon juice

1 Preheat oven to moderately slow.
2 Strain cherries over small bowl. Combine cherry juice with stock, port, cinnamon, cloves and garlic in large baking dish. Place duck on metal rack over baking dish; cover tightly with oiled foil. Roast, covered, in moderately slow oven about 2 hours or until duck meat is tender. Strain pan liquid into large jug; skim away fat.
3 Cut apples into thin slices; cut slices into matchstick-sized pieces. Place apple and seeded cherries in large bowl with nuts, onion, parsley, oil and lemon juice; toss gently to combine salad. Serve duck with salad and cherry sauce.

serves 4
per serving 40g fat; 3001kJ (717 cal)

TIP Do not slice apples until you're ready to assemble the salad or they will discolour.

roasted chicken with 40 cloves of garlic

PREPARATION TIME 20 MINUTES **COOKING TIME** 1 HOUR 20 MINUTES (PLUS STANDING TIME)

This moreish Provençal favourite will surprise you with how mild and creamy the garlic becomes after its long roasting. Feel free to use as many cloves as you want because any leftover roasted garlic cloves can be peeled and used to make a simple garlic mayonnaise known as aioli.

3 bulbs garlic
60g butter, softened
1.5kg chicken
2 teaspoons salt
2 teaspoons cracked black pepper
1 cup (250ml) water

ROASTED POTATOES
1kg tiny new potatoes
cooking-oil spray

1 Preheat oven to moderately hot.
2 Separate cloves from garlic bulb, leaving peel intact. Rub butter over outside of chicken and inside cavity; press combined salt and pepper onto skin and inside cavity. Place half of the garlic inside cavity; tie legs together with kitchen string.
3 Place remaining garlic cloves, in single layer, in medium baking dish; place chicken on garlic. Pour the water carefully into dish; roast chicken, uncovered, in moderately hot oven, brushing occasionally with pan juices, about 1 hour 20 minutes or until browned and cooked through.
4 Meanwhile, make roasted potatoes.
5 Stand chicken on platter, covered with foil, 15 minutes before serving with roasted garlic and potatoes.

ROASTED POTATOES Boil steam or microwave potatoes 5 minutes; drain. Pat dry with absorbent paper; cool 10 minutes. Place potatoes, in single layer, in large oiled baking dish; spray with cooking-oil spray. Roast, uncovered, in moderately hot oven for about the last 30 minutes of chicken cooking time or until potatoes are tender.

serves 4
per serving 42.9g fat; 3009kJ (719 cal)

char-grilled spatchcock on puy lentils

PREPARATION TIME 40 MINUTES **COOKING TIME** 55 MINUTES

Puy lentils are tiny dark green lentils that hold their shape well after having been cooked. Any small green lentil can be substituted for puy lentils.

1 tablespoon olive oil
1 medium brown onion (150g), chopped finely
1 small carrot (70g), chopped finely
1 trimmed celery stalk (100g), chopped finely
1 clove garlic, crushed
1 cup (220g) puy lentils
3½ cups (875ml) chicken stock
4 x 500g spatchcocks
40g butter
2 teaspoons finely chopped fresh thyme
1 cup (250ml) dry white wine

1 Preheat oven to hot.
2 Heat oil in large saucepan; cook onion, carrot, celery and garlic, stirring occasionally, until onion softens. Add lentils and 2 cups of the stock; bring to a boil. Reduce heat; simmer, covered, about 40 minutes or until lentils are just tender.
3 Meanwhile, wash spatchcocks under cold water; pat dry inside and out with absorbent paper. Cut along both sides of backbone of spatchcock; press to flatten. Make a pocket between breast and skin with finger; push a quarter of the combined butter and thyme under skin of each spatchcock. Cook spatchcocks on heated oiled grill plate (or grill or barbecue) about 25 minutes or until spatchcocks are cooked through.
4 Combine wine and remaining stock in small saucepan; bring to a boil. Boil, uncovered, about 20 minutes or until sauce is reduced to about 1 cup. Serve spatchcocks with lentils, drizzle with sauce.

serves 4
per serving 52.4g fat; 3680kJ (879 cal)

Cut along both sides of backbone of spatchcock.

Using both hands, press down on spatchcock breast to flatten.

Push a quarter of the combined butter and thyme under skin.

roasted spatchcock with duck money bags

PREPARATION TIME 30 MINUTES **COOKING TIME** 45 MINUTES

Juniper berries are the dried fruit of the juniper shrub, an evergreen from the Northern Hemisphere, and are found in specialty herb or health food shops. If you are unable to find duck mince, buy a 150g breast and chop it extremely finely yourself.

2 x 500g spatchcocks
40g butter, softened
6 juniper berries, crushed
1 tablespoon fresh
    lemon thyme leaves
1 lemon, quartered
1 tablespoon lemon juice
1 cup (250ml) chicken stock

DUCK MONEY BAGS

20g butter
1 small brown onion (80g),
    chopped finely
2 cloves garlic, crushed
125g duck mince
2 teaspoons finely grated
    lemon rind
1 teaspoon fresh
    lemon thyme leaves
2 sheets fillo pastry
10g butter, melted, extra

1 Preheat oven to moderate.
2 Wash spatchcocks under cold water; pat dry inside and out with absorbent paper.
3 Combine butter, berries and thyme in small bowl. Loosen spatchcock skin; rub butter mixture between skin and flesh and over outside of spatchcocks. Place 2 lemon quarters in cavity of each spatchcock.
4 Place spatchcocks on oiled wired rack over shallow flameproof baking dish; roast, uncovered, in moderate oven about 40 minutes or until browned and cooked through.
5 Meanwhile, make duck money bags.
6 Remove spatchcocks from baking dish; cover to keep warm. Add lemon juice and stock to juices in dish; bring to a boil. Reduce heat; simmer sauce, uncovered, 5 minutes.
7 Halve spatchcocks; place one half on each serving plate along with two money bags, drizzle with sauce. Serve with steamed broccoli, if desired.

DUCK MONEY BAGS Melt butter in large frying pan; cook onion and garlic, stirring, until onion softens. Cool 5 minutes. Combine onion mixture in small bowl with mince, rind and thyme. Brush 1 sheet of fillo with extra melted butter; layer with second sheet. Cut layered fillo sheets into eight 13cm squares. Place 1 level tablespoon of the duck mixture in centre of fillo square, gather corners together to form money bag shape; secure with kitchen string. Repeat process with remaining squares and duck mixture; place money bags on oven tray. Cook money bags, uncovered, in moderate oven about 10 minutes or until cooked through.

serves 4
per serving 54.2g fat; 3140kJ (750 cal)

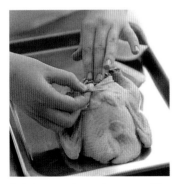

Rub butter mixture between skin and flesh of spatchcock.

pan-fried freshwater trout with cider and brandy sauce

PREPARATION TIME 25 MINUTES **COOKING TIME** 30 MINUTES

Shallots, also called french shallots, golden shallots or eschalots, are small, elongated, brown-skinned members of the onion family that grow in tight clusters similar to garlic.

2 shallots (50g), chopped finely
⅓ cup (80ml) brandy
⅓ cup (80ml) sparkling apple cider
¼ cup (60ml) water
¼ cup (60ml) cream
125g butter, chopped
¼ cup (35g) plain flour
1 teaspoon salt
1 teaspoon cracked black pepper
4 x 150g freshwater trout fillets, boned
1 tablespoon olive oil
80g baby rocket leaves

1 Combine shallot, brandy, cider and the water in medium saucepan; bring to a boil. Reduce heat; simmer, uncovered, about 5 minutes or until almost all liquid evaporates.
2 Add cream to pan; simmer, uncovered, 5 minutes. Add butter, a few pieces at a time, whisking to combine between additions. Strain sauce into medium jug; discard solids. Cover to keep warm.
3 Combine flour, salt and pepper in large shallow dish. Coat fish in flour mixture; shake off excess.
4 Heat oil in large frying pan; cook fish, both sides, until browned lightly and cooked as desired. Divide rocket among serving plates; top with fish, drizzle with sauce.

serves 4
per serving 41.7g fat; 2413kJ (576 cal)

seared salmon with
leek velouté and salmon roe

PREPARATION TIME 30 MINUTES **COOKING TIME** 30 MINUTES

Velouté, a white sauce made from roux (a cooked butter and flour mixture) and stock, is one of the five "mother" sauces in French cooking from which all other sauces are derived. Its particular charm is that the addition of one or two different ingredients changes its character completely. Classic allemande, bercy, crevettes, normande, supreme, and vin blanc sauces are all based on velouté.

3 medium leeks (1kg)
100g butter
2 tablespoons plain flour
½ cup (125ml) dry white wine
1 cup (250ml) chicken stock
1 teaspoon dijon mustard
375g dried egg fettuccine
¼ cup coarsely chopped fresh chervil
1 tablespoon olive oil
6 x 200g salmon fillets
¼ cup (50g) salmon roe

1 Trim cleaned leeks. Cut leeks into 8cm lengths; cut lengths in half lengthways, cut halves into thin strips lengthways.
2 Melt all but 1 tablespoon of the butter in large saucepan; cook leek, stirring occasionally, over medium heat, about 15 minutes or until softened. Stir in flour; cook, stirring, 2 minutes. Gradually stir in wine and stock then mustard; stir until velouté boils and thickens. Cover to keep warm.
3 Meanwhile, cook pasta in large saucepan of boiling water, uncovered, until just tender; drain. Place pasta in large bowl; stir in chervil and remaining butter.
4 Heat oil in large frying pan; cook fish, both sides, until browned lightly and cooked as desired. Divide velouté then pasta among serving plates; top with fish and roe.

serves 6
per serving 32.8g fat; 2986kJ (713 cal)

vegetable pithiviers with roasted tomato sauce

PREPARATION TIME 45 MINUTES **COOKING TIME** 2 HOURS 5 MINUTES

Traditionally an almond-cream flavoured puff pastry dessert, our pithiviers makes its appearance during the savoury part of a meal with its ratatouille-like filling and rich roasted tomato sauce.

10 large egg tomatoes (900g), quartered
2 teaspoons brown sugar
⅓ cup (80ml) olive oil
2 tablespoons red wine vinegar
2 large red capsicums (700g), halved
30g butter
2 large green zucchini (300g), sliced thinly
7 flat mushrooms (560g), sliced thinly
1 clove garlic, crushed
1 tablespoon port
5 sheets ready-rolled puff pastry
1 egg yolk
1 tablespoon milk
50g baby spinach leaves

1 Preheat oven to moderate.
2 Combine tomato, sugar, half of the oil and half of the vinegar in large bowl; place tomato pieces, skin-side down, on oven tray. Roast, uncovered, in moderate oven 1 hour 40 minutes. Remove from oven; return to same bowl; crush with potato masher. Cover to keep warm; reserve tomato sauce.
3 While tomato is roasting, place capsicum, skin-side up, on oven tray. Roast, uncovered, in moderate oven about 40 minutes or until softened. Place capsicum in plastic bag; close tightly, cool. Discard skin, membrane and seeds; slice thinly.
4 Meanwhile, melt butter in large frying pan; cook zucchini, stirring, about 5 minutes or until softened. Place zucchini in small bowl; cover to keep warm. Place mushrooms and garlic in same pan; cook, stirring, about 5 minutes or until mushrooms soften. Add port; cook, stirring, until liquid evaporates.
5 Cut four of the pastry sheets into 16cm squares; cut remaining sheet into quarters. Place one of the small squares on oiled oven tray; centre 9cm cutter on pastry. Layer a quarter of the mushroom mixture, a quarter of the zucchini and a quarter of the capsicum on pastry; remove cutter. Brush border with combined egg yolk and milk; top with one of the large squares, press edges together to seal.
6 Using sharp knife, cut around pithiviers, leaving 5mm border; mark pastry with swirl design from centre to side, taking care not to cut through pastry. Brush lightly with egg mixture. Repeat process with remaining pastry, vegetables and egg mixture. Bake, uncovered, in moderate oven about 25 minutes or until pastry is browned lightly.
7 Meanwhile, combine spinach, remaining oil and remaining vinegar in medium bowl; toss gently to combine. Divide salad among serving plates; serve with pithivier and roasted tomato sauce.

serves 4
per serving 59.3g fat; 3680kJ (879 cal)

Layer a quarter of the vegetables on pastry then remove cutter.

Top vegetables with large pastry square then seal pastry edges.

Using sharp knife, cut around pithivier, leaving 5mm border.

lamb backstraps with vegetable crisps and beurre blanc

PREPARATION TIME 20 MINUTES **COOKING TIME** 35 MINUTES

Beurre blanc, which translates simply as "white butter", is not only wonderful with lamb, but with any meat, poultry or vegetable. Making this sauce is easy if the butter is well-chilled and you make the effort to whisk it continuously to avoid it "splitting".

½ small kumara (125g)
1 small parsnip (120g)
1 large beetroot (200g), trimmed
1 tablespoon olive oil
4 x 200g lamb backstraps
vegetable oil, for deep-frying

BEURRE BLANC
¼ cup (60ml) dry white wine
1 tablespoon lemon juice
¼ cup (60ml) cream
125g cold butter, chopped

1 Using vegetable peeler, slice kumara and parsnip into ribbons. Slice beetroot thinly.
2 Heat olive oil in large frying pan; cook lamb, in batches, about 5 minutes both sides or until cooked as desired. Cover to keep warm.
3 Make beurre blanc.
4 Heat vegetable oil in wok or large saucepan; deep-fry vegetables, in batches, about 2 minutes per batch or until crisp. Drain on absorbent paper.
5 Cut each piece of lamb into three pieces. Divide half of the sauce among serving plates; top with lamb, remaining sauce and vegetable crisps.

BEURRE BLANC Combine wine and juice in medium saucepan; bring to a boil. Boil, without stirring, until reduced by two-thirds. Add cream; return to a boil. Whisk in cold butter, piece by piece, whisking between additions. Pour into medium jug; cover to keep warm.

serves 4
per serving 48g fat; 2780kJ (664 cal)

rolled lamb loin with
tomato concasse and herbed peas

PREPARATION TIME 30 MINUTES **COOKING TIME** 1 HOUR 30 MINUTES

1 medium red capsicum (200g)
700g boned loin of lamb
2 cloves garlic, crushed
20g baby spinach leaves
⅓ cup loosely packed fresh
   basil leaves
1 tablespoon olive oil

TOMATO CONCASSE

1 tablespoon olive oil
3 shallots (75g), chopped finely
4 cloves garlic, crushed
1.2kg large egg tomatoes,
   peeled, seeded, chopped finely
2 tablespoons red wine vinegar

HERBED PEAS

2 cups (240g) frozen peas
2 tablespoons finely chopped
   fresh mint
2 tablespoons finely chopped
   fresh basil
20g butter

1 Preheat oven to very hot. Make tomato concasse.
2 Meanwhile, quarter capsicums; discard seeds and membranes. Roast in very hot oven, skin-side up, until skin blisters and blackens. Cover capsicum in plastic wrap or paper for 5 minutes; peel away skin, then slice capsicum thinly.
3 Reduce oven temperature to moderate. Place lamb, cut-side up, on board; rub garlic into lamb then place capsicum, spinach and basil down centre of lamb; roll tightly, secure at 2cm intervals with kitchen string. Rub oil over lamb roll.
4 Place lamb on wire rack over large shallow baking dish; roast, uncovered, in moderate oven about 1 hour or until lamb is browned and cooked as desired. Cover to keep warm.
5 Make herbed peas.
6 Serve lamb, sliced thickly, with tomato concasse and herbed peas.

TOMATO CONCASSE Heat oil in medium saucepan; cook shallot and garlic, stirring, until shallot softens. Add tomato and vinegar; cook, covered, over low heat, 15 minutes. Uncover; simmer, stirring occasionally, about 30 minutes or until mixture thickens slightly.

HERBED PEAS Cook peas in medium saucepan of boiling water, uncovered, about 2 minutes or until just tender; drain. Combine peas in serving bowl with herbs and butter.

serves 4
per serving 29.2g fat; 2052kJ (490 cal)

pan-fried bream with roasted ratatouille

PREPARATION TIME 20 MINUTES **COOKING TIME** 35 MINUTES

Ratatouille is traditionally a stew-like blend of Mediterranean vegetables prepared in a pan on top the stove over heat. Here, we oven-roast them, and the effect is sensational.

3 large egg tomatoes (270g), peeled, chopped coarsely
2 baby eggplants (120g), sliced thickly
2 medium zucchini (240g), sliced thickly
2 medium red capsicums (400g), chopped coarsely
1 medium red onion (170g), cut into wedges
⅓ cup (80ml) olive oil
2 cloves garlic, crushed
½ cup loosely packed torn fresh basil leaves
1 tablespoon coarsely chopped fresh oregano
8 x 120g bream fillets
50g baby spinach leaves

1 Preheat oven to very hot.
2 Place tomato, eggplant, zucchini, capsicum, onion and one tablespoon of the oil in large baking dish; toss to coat vegetables. Roast, in single layer, uncovered, in very hot oven, stirring occasionally, about 20 minutes or until vegetables are brown and tender. Stir in garlic and herbs.
3 Blend or process 2 cups of the vegetables with 1 tablespoon of the remaining oil until smooth; cover to keep warm.
4 Heat remaining oil in large frying pan; cook fish, in batches, about 2 minutes each side or until cooked as desired. Divide ratatouille puree among serving plates; top with vegetables, fish then spinach.

serves 4
per serving 31g fat; 2157kJ (515 cal)

desserts

blackberry pudding

PREPARATION TIME 20 MINUTES **COOKING TIME** 30 MINUTES (PLUS COOLING AND REFRIGERATION TIME)

3 eggs
½ cup (110g) caster sugar
1 tablespoon cornflour
¾ cup (110g) self-raising flour
1 teaspoon butter
¼ cup (60ml) boiling water
⅓ cup (75g) caster sugar, extra
½ cup (125ml) water
300g frozen blackberries
500g frozen mixed berries
¼ cup (80g) blackberry jam

1 Preheat oven to moderate. Grease 25cm x 30cm swiss roll pan; line with baking paper.

2 Beat eggs in small bowl with electric mixer until thick and creamy. Gradually add sugar, one tablespoon at a time, beating until sugar is dissolved between additions. Transfer to large bowl.

3 Fold triple-sifted flours into egg mixture. Pour combined butter and boiling water down side of bowl; fold into egg mixture. Pour mixture into prepared pan; bake, uncovered, in moderate oven about 15 minutes. Cool cake in pan.

4 Meanwhile, place extra sugar and the water in medium saucepan; bring to a boil. Stir in fruit; return to a boil. Reduce heat; simmer, uncovered, about 3 minutes or until fruit thaws. Strain over medium bowl; reserve syrup and berries separately.

5 Turn cake out onto board. Line 1-litre (4-cup) pudding basin with plastic wrap, extending wrap 10cm over side of basin. Cut circle slightly smaller than top edge of basin from cake using tip of sharp knife; cut second circle exact size of base of basin from cake. Cut remaining cake into 10cm pieces; place small cake circle in base of basin and use pieces to line side of basin. Pour ⅔ cup of the reserved syrup into small jug; reserve. Fill basin with berries; cover with remaining syrup, top with large cake circle. Cover pudding with overhanging plastic wrap, weight pudding with saucer; refrigerate 3 hours or overnight.

6 Stir jam and 2 tablespoons of the reserved syrup in small saucepan until heated through. Turn pudding onto serving plate; brush with remaining reserved syrup then jam mixture. Serve with whipped cream, if desired.

serves 6
per serving 4g fat; 1324kJ (316 cal)

Using sharp knife, cut circle exact size of base of basin from cake.

Cover base and side of pudding basin with cake pieces.

Fill with berries and syrup; top pudding with large cake circle.

chocolate soufflé with raspberry coulis

PREPARATION TIME 15 MINUTES **COOKING TIME** 20 MINUTES

Today, a coulis is generally regarded to be a thick puree or sauce usually made from fruit such as tomatoes or berries; however, the original French culinary use of the word referred to the juices that flow into the pan from meat as it cooks.

1 tablespoon caster sugar
50g butter
1 tablespoon plain flour
200g dark eating
   chocolate, melted
2 egg yolks
4 egg whites
¼ cup (55g) caster sugar, extra

RASPBERRY COULIS
150g frozen raspberries, thawed
2 tablespoons caster sugar
4 cloves
½ cup (125ml) dry red wine

1 Preheat oven to moderately hot. Grease four ¾-cup (180ml) soufflé dishes. Sprinkle insides of dishes evenly with sugar; shake away excess. Place dishes on oven tray.
2 Melt butter in small saucepan, add flour; cook, stirring, about 2 minutes or until mixture thickens and bubbles. Remove from heat; stir in chocolate and egg yolks. Transfer to large bowl.
3 Beat egg whites in small bowl with electric mixer until soft peaks form. Gradually add extra sugar, one tablespoon at a time, beating until sugar dissolves between additions. Fold egg white mixture into chocolate mixture, in two batches.
4 Divide soufflé mixture among prepared dishes; bake, uncovered, in moderately hot oven about 15 minutes or until soufflés are puffed.
5 Meanwhile, make raspberry coulis.
6 Serve soufflés with coulis.

RASPBERRY COULIS Combine raspberries and sugar in small saucepan; cook, without boiling, until sugar dissolves. Add cloves and wine; bring to a boil. Reduce heat; simmer, uncovered, about 5 minutes or until coulis thickens. Strain coulis into medium jug.

serves 4
per serving 27.5g fat; 2277kJ (544 cal)

prune and custard tart

PREPARATION TIME 20 MINUTES (PLUS REFRIGERATION TIME)
COOKING TIME 35 MINUTES (PLUS COOLING AND STANDING TIME)

1½ cups (250g) seeded prunes
2 tablespoons brandy
300ml cream
3 eggs
⅔ cup (150g) caster sugar
1 teaspoon vanilla extract

PASTRY
1¼ cups (175g) plain flour
⅓ cup (55g) icing sugar mixture
¼ cup (30g) almond meal
125g cold butter, chopped
1 egg yolk
1 tablespoon water

1 Make pastry.
2 Reduce oven temperature to slow.
3 Blend or process prunes and brandy until mixture forms a paste; spread into tart shell.
4 Bring cream to a boil in small saucepan; remove from heat. Whisk eggs, sugar and vanilla in small bowl until combined; gradually add cream, whisking continuously until combined. Pour custard into tart shell; bake, uncovered, in slow oven about 20 minutes or until custard just sets. Stand 10 minutes; serve tart warm or cold dusted with icing sugar, if desired.

PASTRY Blend or process flour, sugar, almond meal and butter until mixture is crumbly. Add egg yolk and the water; process until ingredients just come together. Enclose in plastic wrap; refrigerate 30 minutes. Grease 26cm-round loose-base flan tin. Roll pastry between sheets of baking paper until large enough to line prepared tin. Lift pastry into tin; press into side, trim edge, prick base all over with fork. Cover; refrigerate 20 minutes. Preheat oven to moderately hot. Place tin on oven tray; cover pastry with baking paper, fill with dried beans or rice. Bake, uncovered, in moderately hot oven 10 minutes. Remove paper and beans carefully from tin; bake in moderately hot oven about 5 minutes or until tart shell browns lightly. Cool to room temperature.

serves 8
per serving 31.7g fat; 2275kJ (544 cal)

caramelised apple clafoutis

PREPARATION TIME 15 MINUTES **COOKING TIME** 50 MINUTES

Clafoutis is originally from the Limousin region of central France where, in the local dialect, it translates as "brimming over". It is one of the world's easiest desserts to make: a sweet batter is poured into a baking dish "brimming" with cherries, prunes or the fresh fruit of your choice, and baked. How easy – and delicious – is that? Traditionally, cherries native to the region were used, but our version uses golden delicious apples, caramelised then topped with batter.

6 medium apples (900g)
50g unsalted butter
½ cup (110g) firmly packed brown sugar
⅓ cup (75g) caster sugar
⅓ cup (50g) plain flour
⅓ cup (50g) self-raising flour
4 eggs, beaten lightly
⅔ cup (160ml) milk
⅔ cup (160ml) cream
80g unsalted butter, melted, extra
1 teaspoon vanilla extract

1 Preheat oven to moderately hot. Grease shallow 2.5-litre (10-cup) ovenproof dish.
2 Peel, core and halve apples; cut each half into four wedges.
3 Melt butter in large frying pan; cook apple, stirring, about 5 minutes or until browned lightly. Add brown sugar; cook, stirring, about 5 minutes or until mixture thickens slightly. Place apple mixture into prepared dish; cool 5 minutes.
4 Meanwhile, combine caster sugar and flours in medium bowl; make well in centre. Gradually whisk in combined remaining ingredients until smooth. Pour batter over apple mixture; bake, uncovered, in moderately hot oven about 40 minutes. Serve hot with double cream and dust with icing sugar, if desired.

serves 6
per serving 32.6g fat; 2274kJ (543cal)

fresh figs in honey and fennel syrup served with muscat granita

PREPARATION TIME 15 MINUTES **COOKING TIME** 10 MINUTES (PLUS COOLING AND FREEZING TIME)

Muscat is a sweet, aromatic dessert wine, possessing an almost musty flavour. It is made from the fully matured muscatel grape. Tokay, sweet riesling or gewürztraminer can be substituted for the muscat in the granita; drink what remains of the wine with this dessert.

1 cup (250ml) water
½ cup (125ml) muscat
½ cup (110g) caster sugar
1 teaspoon black peppercorns
1 teaspoon finely grated lemon rind
1 tablespoon lemon juice
1 tablespoon fennel seeds
½ cup (125ml) water, extra
¼ cup (90g) honey
8 large fresh figs (640g)

1 Combine the water, muscat, sugar, peppercorns, rind and juice in small saucepan; bring to a boil. Cool 10 minutes; strain into 14cm x 21cm loaf pan. Cover with foil; freeze about 4 hours or until firm, scraping granita from bottom and sides of pan with fork every hour.

2 Dry-fry fennel seeds in small saucepan until fragrant. Add the extra water and honey; bring to a boil. Reduce heat; simmer, uncovered, without stirring, about 5 minutes or until mixture thickens slightly. Strain through sieve into small jug; discard seeds. Cool syrup 10 minutes.

3 Cut figs lengthways into five slices; divide among serving plates, drizzle with syrup, top with granita.

serves 4
per serving 0.5g fat; 1095kJ (262 cal)

pear tarte tatin

PREPARATION TIME 20 MINUTES (PLUS REFRIGERATION TIME)
COOKING TIME 1 HOUR 15 MINUTES (PLUS COOLING TIME)

3 large firm pears (990g)
90g butter, chopped
½ cup (110g) firmly packed brown sugar
⅔ cup (160ml) cream
¼ cup (35g) toasted pecans, chopped coarsely

PASTRY
1¼ cups (175g) plain flour
⅓ cup (55g) icing sugar mixture
90g butter, chopped
1 egg yolk
1 tablespoon water

1 Peel and core pears; cut lengthways into quarters.
2 Melt butter with brown sugar in large frying pan. Add cream, stirring, until sugar dissolves; bring to a boil. Add pear; reduce heat, simmer, turning occasionally, about 45 minutes or until tender.
3 Meanwhile, make pastry.
4 Preheat oven to hot.
5 Place pear, round-side down, in deep 22cm-round cake pan; pour caramelised pan liquid over pear, sprinkle with nuts.
6 Roll pastry between sheets of baking paper until slightly larger than circumference of prepared pan. Remove top paper, turn pastry onto pears. Remove remaining paper; tuck pastry between pears and side of pan. Bake, uncovered, in hot oven about 25 minutes or until pastry is browned lightly. Cool 5 minutes; turn tart onto serving plate, serve with cinnamon-scented whipped cream, if desired.

PASTRY Blend or process flour, icing sugar and butter until mixture is crumbly. Add egg yolk and the water; process until ingredients just come together. Enclose in plastic wrap; refrigerate 30 minutes.

serves 6
per serving 40.7g fat; 2690kJ (643 cal)

ricotta pancakes with vanilla-flavoured quince

PREPARATION TIME 25 MINUTES (PLUS STANDING TIME) **COOKING TIME** 2 HOURS 45 MINUTES

2 small quinces (400g)
1 vanilla bean, halved
3 cups (750ml) water
1½ cups (330g) caster sugar
¾ cup (150g) ricotta cheese
2 eggs, separated
½ teaspoon vanilla extract
1 tablespoon caster sugar, extra
2 tablespoons milk
2 tablespoons self-raising flour
10g butter

1 Peel and core quinces; cut each quince into four slices widthways.
2 Halve vanilla bean lengthways, combine in medium saucepan with the water and sugar, stirring, until sugar dissolves; bring to a boil. Add quince, reduce heat; simmer, covered, about 1½ hours. Uncover; simmer, stirring occasionally, about 1 hour or until quince is tender and syrup rosy-pink in colour. Discard vanilla bean.
3 Meanwhile, beat cheese in medium bowl with electric mixer until smooth; beat in egg yolks, vanilla, extra sugar, milk and flour until smooth. Stand 15 minutes.
4 Beat egg whites in small bowl until firm peaks form; fold egg whites, in two batches, into cheese mixture.
5 Melt butter in large non-stick frying pan; using 2 tablespoons of batter for each pancake, cook two pancakes at a time, uncovered, until bubbles appear on the surface. Turn; cook until browned lightly. Remove pancakes from pan; cover to keep warm. Repeat process with remaining batter to make a total of eight pancakes.
6 Place two pancakes on each serving plate; top each with a slice of quince, drizzle with syrup.

serves 4
per serving 9.6g fat; 2105kJ (503 cal)

mille-feuille with almonds and raspberries

PREPARATION TIME 25 MINUTES **COOKING TIME** 15 MINUTES (PLUS REFRIGERATION AND COOLING TIME)

Mille-feuille, pronounced meal-fwee, translates as "thousand leaves", and refers to puff pasty used in multi-layered sweet or savoury dishes. We've adapted the classic dessert version here by layering fillo pastry with almonds and honey.

1⅓ cups (330ml) milk
4 egg yolks
½ cup (110g) caster sugar
2 tablespoons plain flour
1 tablespoon cornflour
1 teaspoon vanilla extract
50g butter
1 tablespoon honey
2 sheets fillo pastry
⅓ cup (55g) toasted blanched almonds, chopped finely
¾ cup (180ml) thickened cream
300g raspberries

1 Bring milk to a boil in medium saucepan. Combine egg yolks, sugar, flours and vanilla in medium bowl; gradually whisk in hot milk. Return custard mixture to same pan; stir, over heat, until mixture boils and thickens. Return custard to same bowl, cover; refrigerate about 1 hour or until cold.
2 Meanwhile, combine butter and honey in same cleaned pan; stir, over low heat, until smooth.
3 Preheat oven to moderately hot. Grease two oven trays.
4 Brush one fillo sheet with half of the honey mixture; sprinkle with nuts. Top with remaining fillo sheet; brush with remaining honey mixture. Cut fillo stack into 7cm-squares; place squares on prepared trays. Bake, uncovered, in moderately hot oven about 5 minutes or until browned lightly. Cool 10 minutes.
5 Meanwhile, beat cream in small bowl with electric mixer until soft peaks form; fold into cold custard mixture. Place one pastry square on each serving plate; top each with one heaped tablespoon of the custard mixture and a few raspberries. Place second pastry square on each; repeat with another layer of custard and raspberries then top each with third pastry square. Serve mille-feuilles with remaining raspberries; dust with icing sugar, if desired.

serves 8
per serving 22g fat; 1372kJ (328 cal)

DESSERTS

poached plums with almond milk ice-cream

PREPARATION TIME 20 MINUTES **COOKING TIME** 40 MINUTES (PLUS STANDING AND FREEZING TIME)

2 cups (500ml) water
½ cup (70g) toasted slivered almonds
1 vanilla bean
300ml cream
¾ cup (165g) caster sugar
6 egg yolks

POACHED PLUMS
2 cups (500ml) water
1 cup (250ml) port
½ cup (110g) caster sugar
1 cinnamon stick
4 plums (450g), halved, seeded

1 Blend or process the water and nuts until fine. Strain almond milk through a muslin-lined strainer into medium saucepan; discard solids.
2 Halve vanilla bean lengthways, scrape seeds into pan with almond milk. Add pod with cream and ¼ cup of the sugar to pan; bring to a boil. Remove from heat; stand 30 minutes. Discard pod.
3 Meanwhile, preheat oven to moderate. Line 14cm x 21cm loaf pan with baking paper.
4 Beat egg yolks and remaining sugar in medium bowl with electric mixer until thick and creamy. Gradually stir in almond milk mixture; return to same pan. Cook, stirring over low heat, until mixture thickens slightly. Remove from heat; cool to room temperature. Pour ice-cream mixture into prepared loaf pan, cover with foil; freeze until firm.
5 Remove ice-cream from freezer, turn into large bowl; chop ice-cream coarsely then beat with electric mixer until smooth. Return to loaf pan, cover; freeze until firm.
6 Meanwhile, make poached plums.
7 Slice ice-cream into four pieces; divide among serving plates. Top with plums and syrup.

POACHED PLUMS Stir the water, port, sugar and cinnamon in medium saucepan, without boiling, until sugar dissolves. Add plums; cook, uncovered, over low heat, about 30 minutes or until just tender. Remove plums from syrup; discard skins. Bring syrup to a boil; boil, uncovered, about 10 minutes or until syrup is reduced to about 1 cup. Remove from heat, discard cinnamon; cool 10 minutes. Refrigerate, covered, until cold.

serves 4
per serving 46.7g fat; 3563kJ (851 cal)

112

chocolate marquise

PREPARATION TIME 30 MINUTES **COOKING TIME** 15 MINUTES (PLUS REFRIGERATION AND FREEZING TIME)

A marquise is based on the classic french bavarois (bavarian cream), a cold dessert composed of a rich egg custard, whipped cream and any of a number of flavourings, the choice being up to the cook – chocolate being our favourite. The chocolate sponge roll in this recipe is made with plain as opposed to self-raising flour because the beaten eggs are enough to aerate the mixture.

¾ cup (180ml) thickened cream
100g dark eating chocolate, chopped coarsely
4 egg yolks
2 eggs
½ cup (110g) caster sugar
300ml thickened cream, extra
¼ cup (60ml) orange-flavoured liqueur
¾ cup (75g) coarsely grated dark eating chocolate
2 teaspoons finely grated orange rind

CHOCOLATE SPONGE

4 eggs
⅔ cup (150g) caster sugar
⅓ cup (50g) plain flour
1 tablespoon cocoa powder

1 Make chocolate sponge.

2 Line base and long sides of 14cm x 21cm loaf pan with baking paper. Cut two rectangles from cooled sponge, one measuring 13cm x 21cm, the other 11cm x 19cm; discard remaining sponge.

3 Combine cream and chopped chocolate in small saucepan; stir over low heat until smooth. Beat egg yolks, eggs and sugar in medium bowl with electric mixer until thick and creamy; with motor operating, gradually beat hot chocolate mixture into egg mixture. Cover; refrigerate about 30 minutes or until mixture thickens slightly.

4 Meanwhile, beat extra cream in small bowl with electric mixer until soft peaks form; fold cream, liqueur, grated chocolate and rind into cooled chocolate mixture.

5 Place smaller rectangle of sponge in prepared pan; pour in chocolate mixture, top with remaining sponge rectangle. Cover with foil; freeze until firm. Turn marquise out onto board; stand at room temperature about 5 minutes or until softened slightly. Slice thickly, serve with fresh berries macerated in the same orange-flavoured liqueur, if desired.

CHOCOLATE SPONGE Preheat oven to moderate. Grease 25cm x 30cm swiss roll pan; line base with baking paper. Beat eggs and sugar in small bowl with electric mixer until thick and creamy; transfer to large bowl. Fold in triple-sifted combined flour and cocoa; spread mixture into prepared pan. Bake, uncovered, in moderate oven about 10 minutes. Cool 10 minutes.

serves 10
per serving 28.4g fat; 1978kJ (473 cal)

glossary

ALMONDS pointy-ended, flat nuts with pitted brown shell enclosing a creamy white kernel, which is covered by a brown skin.
blanched brown skins removed.
meal also known as ground almonds; nuts are powdered to a coarse flour texture. For use in baking or as a thickening agent.
slivered small pieces cut lengthways.

BACON RASHERS also known as slices of bacon; made from pork side, cured and smoked.

BAKING POWDER a raising agent consisting mainly of two parts cream of tartar to one part bicarbonate of soda (baking soda).

BASIL an aromatic herb; there are many types, but the most commonly used is sweet basil.

BAY LEAVES aromatic leaves from the bay tree used to flavour soups, stocks and casseroles.

BEETROOT also known as red beets; firm, round root vegetable. Can be eaten raw in salads, boiled and sliced, or roasted then mashed like potatoes.

BREADCRUMBS packaged, fine-textured, crunchy, purchased white breadcrumbs.
stale 1- or 2-day-old bread made into crumbs by blending or processing.

BRIOCHE rich yeast-risen bread made with butter and eggs. Available from pâtisseries or specialty bread shops.

BROCCOLINI a cross between broccoli and chinese kale; is milder and sweeter than broccoli. Each long stem is topped by a loose floret that closely resembles broccoli; it is completely edible.

BUTTER use salted or unsalted ("sweet") butter; 125g is equal to 1 stick butter.

BUTTERMILK sold alongside fresh milk products in supermarkets; is commercially made by a method similar to yogurt. Despite the implication of its name, it is low in fat and is a good substitute for dairy products such as cream or sour cream.

CAPERS the grey-green buds of a warm climate (usually Mediterranean) shrub; sold either dried and salted or pickled in a vinegar brine. Baby capers are small, fuller-flavoured and more expensive than the full-size ones. Capers, whether packed in brine or in salt, must be rinsed well before using.

CAPSICUM also known as bell pepper or, simply, pepper. Discard seeds and membranes before use.

CARDAMOM native to India and used extensively in its cuisine; this spice can be purchased in pod, seed or ground form.

CAYENNE PEPPER a thin-fleshed, extremely hot red chilli dried and ground.

CELERIAC tuberous root with brown skin, white flesh and a celery-like flavour.

CHEESE
blue mould-treated cheeses mottled with blue veining. Varieties include firm and crumbly Stilton types to mild, creamy brie-like cheeses.
goat made from goats milk; has an earthy, strong taste. It is available in both soft and firm textures, and in various shapes and sizes. Can sometimes be sold rolled in ash or herbs.
gruyère a swiss cheese having small holes and a nutty, slightly salty, flavour.
parmesan a sharp-tasting, dry, hard cheese; made from skim or part-skim milk, and aged for at least a year.
ricotta a sweet, moist cheese with a fat content of around 8.5% and a slightly grainy texture.

CHERRIES soft stone fruit varying in colour from yellow to dark red. Sweet cherries are eaten whole and in desserts, while sour cherries, such as the bitter Morello variety, are used in jams, preserves, pies and savoury dishes, particularly as an accompaniment to game birds and meats.

CHERVIL also known as cicily; fennel-flavoured herb with curly dark-green leaves.

CHIVES related to the onion and leek, with subtle onion flavour.
garlic chives, also known as chinese chives, are strongly flavoured, have flat leaves, and are usually eaten in stir-fries.

CINNAMON STICK dried inner bark of the shoots of the cinnamon tree.

CLOVES dried flower buds of a tropical tree; used whole or ground. Has a distinctively pungent and "spicy" scent and flavour.

COCOA POWDER also known as cocoa; dried, unsweetened, roasted, then ground, cocoa beans.

CONFIT from the French verb meaning "to preserve", confit is most commonly thought to be a culinary term applied to fowl or pork slow-cooked and preserved in fat; however, the name can apply to any foodstuff, from meats to fruits and vegetables, cooked in any auxiliary ingredient, from sugar (confiture) to butter, that assists in its keeping qualities.

CORNFLOUR also known as cornstarch; used as a thickening agent in cooking.

CORNICHON French for gherkin, a very small variety of pickled cucumber. Are a traditional accompaniment to pâté or as a condiment to salads.

CRÈME FRAÎCHE mature fermented cream having a slightly tangy, nutty flavour and velvety texture. Used in savoury and sweet dishes.

DIJON MUSTARD a pale brown, distinctively flavoured, fairly mild french mustard.

EGG some recipes in this book call for raw or barely cooked eggs; exercise caution if salmonella is a problem in your area.

EGGPLANT also known as aubergine. Can also be purchased char-grilled in jars.

FENNEL also known as finocchio or anise; eaten raw in salads or braised or fried as a vegetable accompaniment. Also the name given to dried seeds having a liquorice flavour.

FLOUR
plain an all-purpose flour, made from wheat.
self-raising plain flour sifted with baking powder in the proportion of 1 cup flour to 2 teaspoons baking powder.

GRAVY BEEF boneless stewing beef, which when slow cooked, imbues stocks, soups and casseroles with a mild, yet redolent, flavour.

HORSERADISH CREAM a commercially prepared creamy paste made of grated horseradish, vinegar, oil and sugar.

JAM also known as preserve or conserve; usually made from fruit.

JUNIPER BERRIES dried fruit from the evergreen tree of the same name; provides the distinctive flavour to gin.

KITCHEN STRING made of a natural product, such as cotton or hemp, so that it neither affects the flavour of the food it's tied around nor melts when heated.

KUMARA Polynesian name of orange-fleshed sweet potato; often confused with yam.

LAMINGTON PAN 20cm x 30cm slab cake pan, 3cm deep.

LEEK a member of the onion family. Resembles the green shallot, but is much larger.

MARYLAND leg and thigh of fowl still connected in a single piece with bones and skin intact.

MAYONNAISE we use whole-egg mayonnaise in our recipes.

MERGUEZ small, spicy sausage traditionally made with lamb; recognised by its chilli-red colour. Found in butchers, delicatessens and sausage specialty stores.

MESCLUN is a salad mix of assorted young lettuce and other green leaves.

MINCE MEAT also known as ground meat.

MUSCAT a sweet, fruity dessert wine, made from the grape of the same name; is almost caramel in colour.

MUSHROOM
button small, cultivated white mushrooms with a mild flavour.
flat large, flat mushrooms with a rich, earthy flavour; ideal for barbecuing and filling. They are sometimes misnamed field mushrooms, which are wild mushrooms.
oyster also known as abalone; a grey-white mushroom shaped like a fan. Prized for their smooth texture and subtle, oyster-like flavour.
shiitake when fresh also known as chinese black, forest or golden oak; are large and meaty. Have the earthiness and taste of wild mushrooms. When dried, are known as donko or dried chinese mushrooms; rehydrate before use.
swiss brown light to dark brown mushrooms with full-bodied flavour; also known as roman or cremini. Button or cap mushrooms can be substituted.

OIL
olive made from ripe olives. Extra virgin and virgin are the most fully flavoured.
peanut pressed from peanuts; able to handle high heat without burning.
vegetable oils sourced from plants rather than animal fats.

ONIONS
brown and white are interchangeable. Their pungent flesh adds flavour to a vast range of dishes.
green also known as scallion or (incorrectly) shallot; an immature onion picked before the bulb has formed, having a long, bright-green edible stalk.
pickling also known as cocktail onions; are brown baby onions, larger than shallots. Used raw pickled in brine or cooked in stews and casseroles.
shallots also called french shallots, golden shallots or eschalots; brown-skinned, small, elongated member of the onion family.
red also known as spanish, red spanish or bermuda onion; a sweet-flavoured, large, purple-red onion.

ORANGE-FLAVOURED LIQUEUR You can use Cointreau, Grand Marnier, Curaçao or any other orange-flavoured liqueur.

OSSO BUCO another name used by butchers for veal shin; usually cut into 3cm- to 5cm-thick slices.

PARSLEY, FLAT-LEAF also known as continental parsley or italian parsley.

PASTRY
fillo also known as phyllo; tissue-thin pastry sheets purchased chilled or frozen.
puff, ready-rolled packaged sheets of frozen puff pastry, available from supermarkets.

PATTY-PAN SQUASH also known as crookneck or custard marrow pumpkins; round, slightly flat, yellow to pale green in colour with a scalloped edge. Harvested young, it has firm white flesh and a distinct flavour.

PECANS a golden-brown, rich, buttery nut.

PEPPERCORNS
black picked when berry is not quite ripe; strongest flavoured of all peppercorns.
green soft, unripe berry of the pepper plant, usually sold packed in brine.

PISTACHIOS pale green, delicately flavoured nut inside hard off-white shell. To peel, soak shelled nuts in boiling water for about 5 minutes; drain, then pat dry with absorbent paper. Rub skins with cloth to peel.

POLENTA a flour-like cereal made of ground corn (maize); similar to cornmeal, but finer and lighter. Also the name of the dish made from it.

PRUNES commercially or sun-dried plums.

PUMPKIN used interchangeably with the word squash, pumpkin is a member of the gourd family. Various types can be substituted for one another.
butternut a pear-shaped pumpkin with golden skin and orange flesh.

QUAIL also known as partridge; small, delicate flavoured, domestically grown game birds ranging in weight from 250g to 300g.

QUINCE yellow-skinned fruit with hard texture and astringent, tart taste.

REDCURRANT JELLY a preserve made from redcurrants; used as a glaze for desserts and meats or in sauces.

ROCKET also known as arugula, rugula or rucola; a peppery-tasting green leaf. Baby rocket leaves are smaller and less peppery.

SAVOY CABBAGE large, heavy head with crinkled dark-green outer leaves; a fairly mild-tasting cabbage.

SPATCHCOCK a small chicken (poussin), no more than 6 weeks old, weighing a maximum 500g. Also, a cooking technique where a small chicken is split open, then flattened and grilled.

SPLIT PEAS also known as field peas, green or yellow pulse grown for drying; split in half along a centre seam.

SUGAR we used coarse, granulated table sugar, also known as crystal sugar, unless otherwise specified.

brown a soft, fine granulated sugar retaining molasses for its characteristic colour and flavour.
caster also known as superfine or finely granulated table sugar.
icing mixture also known as confectioners' sugar or powdered sugar; pulverised granulated sugar crushed together with a small amount (about 3%) cornflour added.

SWEETBREADS the thymus glands from veal, lamb and pork. They are very perishable, so cook within a day of purchase.

TOMATO
cherry small and round; also known as Tiny Tim or Tom Thumb.
egg also known as Plum or Roma; are smallish and oval-shaped.
paste triple-concentrated tomato puree used to flavour soups, stews, sauces and casseroles.

VANILLA
bean dried, long, thin pod; the minuscule black seeds inside are used to impart a luscious vanilla flavour in baking and desserts. A whole bean can be placed in the sugar container to make the vanilla sugar often called for in recipes.
extract vanilla beans that have been submerged in alcohol. Vanilla essence is not a suitable substitute.

VINEGAR
balsamic made from a regional wine of white Trebbiano grapes that have been specially processed and aged in antique wooden casks, which give it an exquisite pungent flavour.
red wine based on fermented red wine.
white wine made from white wine.

WATERCRESS member of the cress family. Highly perishable, so must be used as soon as possible after puchase.

WITLOF also known as chicory or belgian endive.

ZUCCHINI also known as courgette.

index

facts + figures

Wherever you live, you'll be able to use our recipes with the help of these easy-to-follow conversions. While these conversions are approximate only, the difference between an exact and the approximate conversion of various liquid and dry measures is but minimal, and will not affect your cooking results.

liquid measures

metric	imperial
30ml	1 fluid oz
60ml	2 fluid oz
100ml	3 fluid oz
125ml	4 fluid oz
150ml	5 fluid oz (¼ pint/1 gill)
190ml	6 fluid oz
250ml	8 fluid oz
300ml	10 fluid oz (½ pint)
500ml	16 fluid oz
600ml	20 fluid oz (1 pint)
1000ml (1 litre)	1¾ pints

dry measures

metric	imperial
15g	½oz
30g	1oz
60g	2oz
90g	3oz
125g	4oz (¼lb)
155g	5oz
185g	6oz
220g	7oz
250g	8oz (½lb)
280g	9oz
315g	10oz
345g	11oz
375g	12oz (¾lb)
410g	13oz
440g	14oz
470g	15oz
500g	16oz (1lb)
750g	24oz (1½lb)
1kg	32oz (2lb)

helpful measures

metric	imperial
3mm	⅛in
6mm	¼in
1cm	½in
2cm	¾in
2.5cm	1in
5cm	2in
6cm	2½in
8cm	3in
10cm	4in
13cm	5in
15cm	6in
18cm	7in
20cm	8in
23cm	9in
25cm	10in
28cm	11in
30cm	12in (1ft)

measuring equipment

The difference between one country's measuring cups and another's is, at most, within a 2 or 3 teaspoon variance. (For the record, one Australian metric measuring cup holds approximately 250ml.) The most accurate way of measuring dry ingredients is to weigh them. When measuring liquids, use a clear glass or plastic jug with metric markings. (One Australian metric tablespoon holds 20ml; one Australian metric teaspoon holds 5ml.)

how to measure

When using graduated metric measuring cups, shake dry ingredients loosely into the appropriate cup. Do not tap the cup on a bench or tightly pack the ingredients unless directed to do so. Level top of measuring cups and measuring spoons with a knife. When measuring liquids, place a clear glass or plastic jug with metric markings on a flat surface to check accuracy at eye level.

Note: North America, NZ and the UK use 15ml tablespoons. All cup and spoon measurements are level.

We use large eggs having an average weight of 60g.

oven temperatures

These oven temperatures are only a guide. Always check the manufacturer's manual.

	°C (Celsius)	°F (Fahrenheit)	Gas Mark
Very slow	120	250	½
Slow	140 – 150	275 – 300	1 – 2
Moderately slow	170	325	3
Moderate	180 – 190	350 – 375	4 – 5
Moderately hot	200	400	6
Hot	220 – 230	425 – 450	7 – 8
Very hot	240	475	9

Are you missing some of the
world's favourite cookbooks?

The Australian Women's Weekly cookbooks are available from bookshops, cookshops, supermarkets and other stores all over the world. You can also buy direct from the publisher, using the order form below.

Title	RRP	Qty	Title	RRP	Qty
Almost Vegetarian	£5.99		French Food, New	£5.99	
Asian, Meals in Minutes	£5.99		Get Real, Make a Meal	£5.99	
Babies & Toddlers Good Food	£5.99		Good Food Fast	£5.99	
Barbecue Meals In Minutes (Sep 04)	£5.99		Great Beef Cookbook	£5.99	
Basic Cooking Class	£5.99		Great Chicken Cookbook	£5.99	
Beginners Cooking Class	£5.99		Great Lamb Cookbook	£5.99	
Beginners Simple Meals	£5.99		Greek Cooking Class	£5.99	
Beginners Thai	£5.99		Healthy Heart Cookbook	£5.99	
Best Ever Slimmers' Recipes	£5.99		Indian Cooking Class	£5.99	
Best Food	£5.99		Italian Cooking Class	£5.99	
Best Food Desserts	£5.99		Japanese Cooking Class	£5.99	
Best Food Mains	£5.99		Kids' Birthday Cakes	£5.99	
Big Book of Beautiful Biscuits	£5.99		Kids Cooking (Jul 04)	£5.99	
Biscuits & Slices	£5.99		Lean Food	£5.99	
Cakes & Slices Cookbook	£5.99		Low-fat Feasts	£5.99	
Cakes Cooking Class	£5.99		Low-fat Food For Life	£5.99	
Caribbean Cooking	£5.99		Low-fat Meals in Minutes	£5.99	
Casseroles	£5.99		Main Course Salads	£5.99	
Celebration Cakes	£5.99		Meals in Minutes	£5.99	
Chicken Meals in Minutes	£5.99		Mediterranean Cookbook	£5.99	
Chinese Cooking Class	£5.99		Middle Eastern Cooking Class	£5.99	
Christmas Book	£5.99		Midweek Meals in Minutes	£5.99	
Christmas Cooking (Nov 04)	£5.99		Muffins, Scones & Bread	£5.99	
Cocktails	£5.99		New Finger Food	£5.99	
Cooking for Crowds	£5.99		Pasta Cookbook	£5.99	
Cooking for Friends	£5.99		Pasta Meals in Minutes	£5.99	
Cooking For Two	£5.99		Potatoes	£5.99	
Creative Cooking on a Budget	£5.99		Quick Meals in Minutes	£5.99	
Dinner Beef	£5.99		Quick-mix Biscuits & Slices	£5.99	
Dinner Lamb (Apr 05)	£5.99		Quick-mix Cakes	£5.99	
Dinner Seafood	£5.99		Salads:Simple, Fast & Fresh	£5.99	
Easy Australian Style	£5.99		Saucery	£5.99	
Easy Curry	£5.99		Sensational Stir-Fries	£5.99	
Easy Spanish-Style	£5.99		Short-order Cook	£5.99	
Easy Vietnamese-Style	£5.99		Sweet Old Fashioned Favourites	£5.99	
Essential Barbecue	£5.99		Thai Cooking Class	£5.99	
Essential Microwave	£5.99		Vegetarian Meals in Minutes	£5.99	
Essential Soup	£5.99		Weekend Cook	£5.99	
Freezer, Meals from the	£5.99		Wicked Sweet Indulgences	£5.99	
French Cooking Class	£5.99		Wok, Meals in Minutes	£5.99	
			Total Cost:	£	

Mr/Mrs/Ms _____

Address _____

_____

Postcode _____ Country _____

Daytime phone ( ) _____

I enclose my cheque/money order

for £ _____

OR: please charge my

☐ Access ☐ Visa ☐ Mastercard

Cardholder's name _____

Card number

Expiry date ____ / ____

Cardholder's signature _____

To order: Mail or fax — photocopy or complete the order form above, and send your credit card details or cheque payable to: Australian Consolidated Press (UK), Moulton Park Business Centre, Red House Road, Moulton Park, Northampton NN3 6AQ, phone (+44) (0) 1604 497531, fax (+44) (0) 1604 497533, e-mail books@acpuk.com

Non-UK residents: We accept the credit cards listed on the coupon, or cheques, drafts or International Money Orders payable in sterling and drawn on a UK bank. Credit card charges are at the exchange rate current at the time of payment.

Postage and packing: Within the UK, add £1.50 for one book or £3.00 for two books. There is no postal charge for orders of three or more books for delivery within the UK. For delivery outside the UK, please phone, fax or e-mail for a quote.

Offer ends 31.12.2004

Test Kitchen Staff
Food director *Pamela Clark*
Food editor *Karen Hammial*
Assistant food editor *Amira Georgy*
Test kitchen manager *Kimberley Coverdale*
Senior home economist *Cathie Lonnie*
Home economists *Sammie Coryton, Kelly Cruickshanks, Christina Martignago, Sharon Reeve, Susie Riggall, Kirrily Smith, Kate Tait, Vanessa Vetter*
Editorial coordinator *Rebecca Steyns*
Nutritional Information *Laila Ibram*

ACP Books Staff
Editorial director *Susan Tomnay*
Creative director *Hieu Chi Nguyen*
Senior editor *Wendy Bryant*
Designer *Hieu Chi Nguyen*
Studio manager *Caryl Wiggins*
Editorial/sales coordinator *Caroline Lowry*
Editorial assistant *Karen Lai*
Publishing manager (sales) *Brian Cearnes*
Publishing manager (rights & new projects) *Jane Hazell*
Brand manager *Donna Gianniotis*
Pre-press *Harry Palmer*
Production manager *Carol Currie*
Business manager *Seymour Cohen*
Assistant business analyst *Martin Howes*
Chief executive officer *John Alexander*
Group publisher *Pat Ingram*
Publisher *Sue Wannan*

Produced by ACP Books, Sydney.
Printed by Dai Nippon Printing in Korea.
Published by ACP Publishing Pty Limited, 54 Park St, Sydney; GPO Box 4088, Sydney, NSW 2001.
Ph: (02) 9282 8618 Fax: (02) 9267 9438.
acpbooks@acp.com.au
www.acpbooks.com.au
To order books, phone 136 116.
Send recipe enquiries to:
recipeenquiries@acp.com.au
AUSTRALIA: Distributed by Network Services, GPO Box 4088, Sydney, NSW 2001.
Ph: (02) 9282 8777 Fax: (02) 9264 3278.
UNITED KINGDOM: Distributed by Australian Consolidated Press (UK), Moulton Park Business Centre, Red House Rd, Moulton Park, Northampton, NN3 6AQ.
Ph: (01604) 497 531 Fax: (01604) 497 533
acpukltd@aol.com
CANADA: Distributed by Whitecap Books Ltd, 351 Lynn Ave, North Vancouver, BC, V7J 2C4.
Ph: (604) 980 9852 Fax: (604) 980 8197
customerservice@whitecap.ca
www.whitecap.ca
NEW ZEALAND: Distributed by Netlink Distribution Company, ACP Media Centre, Cnr Fanshawe and Beaumont Streets, Westhaven, Auckland.
PO Box 47906, Ponsonby, Auckland, NZ.
Ph: (09) 366 9966 ask@ndcnz.co.nz

Clark, Pamela.
The Australian Women's Weekly
New French Food.

Includes index.
ISBN 1 86396 360 X
1. Cookery, French.
I. Title. II. Title: New French Food.
III. Title: Australian Women's Weekly.

641.5944
© ACP Publishing Pty Limited 2004
ABN 18 053 273 546

This publication is copyright. No part of it may be reproduced or transmitted in any form without the written permission of the publishers.

The publishers would like to thank the following for props used in photography:
Hale Imports Pty Ltd, Brookvale, NSW;
Thonet, Darlinghurst, NSW.